For Adey

SENSING THE PASSION

REFLECTIONS DURING LENT

KEVIN SCULLY

UPPER
ROOM BOOKS®
NASHVILLE

Original edition published in 1997 by Triangle SPCK, Holy Trinity Church, Marylebone Road,
London NW1 4DU, UK. E-mail: spck@spck.org.uk.
Copyright © 1997 Kevin Scully.

Questions for Reflection and Discussion by Linda Douty.

The Upper Room® Web site http://www.upperroom.org

Cover Design: Uttley/DouPonce DesignWorks, Sisters, OR
Cover Art: Private Collection, Texas/SuperStock
First printing: 2000

Library of Congress Cataloging-in-Publication Data

Scully, Kevin, 1955–

   Sensing the passion : reflections during Lent / by Kevin Scully.

     p. cm.

ISBN: 0-8358-0917-X

   1. Jesus Christ—Passion. 2. Lent—Meditations. I. Title.

BT431.S38 2000

242'.34—dc21   00-022130

Printed in the United States of America

Contents

Foreword

The story of the Passion of Our Lord Jesus Christ is superficially so familiar that there is a danger, as Coleridge perceived, of its "lying bedridden in the dormitory of the soul." So every year Christian people seek with simple attention to enter more profoundly into this story and discover its freshness and power.

These meditations by Kevin Scully are an aid to this renewed encounter. In the springtime of the Church, Christians were well aware that it was important to engage with the story of Jesus Christ with all their created being—heart, mind and soul. They knew that a mere cerebral reading does not disclose the mystery. When the Saints were depicted in early Christian icons it is significant that their nostrils were prominent and their ears were large. This was so they could detect the fragrance of goodness and the stench of evil and listen deeply to the still small voice of God. It is equally significant that their mouths were often painted very small because the great educator is silence and stillness.

Alas, many of these lessons that were clear to early Christians have been forgotten by a Church in which understanding is commonly interpreted solely in cerebral terms. The author provides useful exercises at the end of each chapter to help train us in true spiritual awareness.

I sincerely hope that his book will encourage deep contemplation, leading us all beyond the mere hearing of a narrative into the full reverberation of its truth in our lives.

RICHARD LONDIN

THE RIGHT REVEREND RICHARD CHARTRES

BISHOP OF LONDON

Introduction

This book is something of a nonsense. It is almost the opposite of its title—*Sensing the Passion*. We will focus on the final hours of Jesus Christ by choosing some events for their sentient power. By looking at the Passion of Jesus in such a relatively isolated way, I am asking you to commit a "non-sensical" act.

Why is it non-sensical? In each chapter of what follows we will look at the Passion through one sense only. We will progress through sight, sound, smell, touch and taste. And with each progression we will lose another sensation. But losing a sensory power, or indeed gaining one, does not make a person any less a person. A person is whole, complete, irrespective of the number of functioning faculties.

And yet the senses, each of the five of them, can add to a whole person. They do not necessarily add up to a person but each one can provide something extra. Much of our lives is spent in the reception of and making sense of sentient data:

Do you see that?
What can we hear?
What is that smell?
How does that feel?
What is that taste?

These are the experiences, the raw data, of a sentient being. They are not, they cannot be, complete in themselves. A deaf person is no less a person because of the lack of hearing. Nor is someone confined to a wheelchair any less human because of a loss of mobility.

Humanity, personhood, is the *whole* being. Senses contribute to it but they do not constitute it. Yet death, the end of physical life, is pronounced when the senses stop. Dead people hear nothing, see nothing, feel nothing, taste nothing, smell nothing. The movement from life to death is the loss of all senses. It is a movement from sense to non-sense. It is a movement from being, in this realm, to nonbeing. This is the movement of every person.

The importance of the senses in the Passion of Jesus is vital. They link us to the Savior. Jesus' experiences were complete human experiences. Jesus' senses were complete human senses. Jesus' sight was like our sight. Jesus' hearing was like our hearing. Jesus' touch was like our touch. Jesus' sense of smell was like ours. Jesus' taste was like our taste.

The Christian story depends on this. But we must act with an intellectual and imaginative caution. That caution stems from our knowledge of the events which we will ponder. Centuries of the retelling of the Passion narratives and church teaching on its significance should lead us to a certain detachment, even when our attention is engaged by the pain and torture involved in the final hours of Jesus.

There is a necessary transformation in the stories of Jesus' life and death. We need to remember this because, without the transformation, the Passion can all too often remain for us unchecked, unmitigated pain and anguish. All these meditations should be then cast in that fuller knowledge of the freedom achieved through the death of Christ. We also realize that the transformation of this suffering lies in the resurrection, which is not part of the Passion itself but integral to our embracing of it.

But there is another possible pitfall. In order to avoid the anguish, one can concentrate solely on the positive consequences of the Passion. These consequences are quite rightly emphasized in the doctrine of the atonement. The doctrine informs us that the death of Jesus is the saving act for all humanity and that through the Passion, Christ took on the sin of the whole world. Jesus' death freed from their sins all those who live on and in the world, and transformed them and it.

Our hesitancy tells us that to concentrate on the efficacy without the painful reality is likewise a false gesture. It is a turning away. It seeks the comfortable by excluding the implications of the complete story. That saving transformation is more than important. It is essential to the Christian story. But it gains its importance, as much of Christianity gains its power, by virtue of a simple fact. We do know the full story.

For instance, we know the pain that lies ahead for the family of Jesus when the protagonists are still celebrating the joy of Jesus' birth. We know, in a way that Joseph and Mary and the shepherds could not, that beyond the magnificent celebration at Bethlehem is an extraordinary future. We know that when this child was to grow Jesus would be a miracle worker, a teacher, then later be accused, betrayed and die a cruel death upon a cross.

Yet we know much more than that. We know of Jesus' lying in the tomb, Jesus' appearances after death, Jesus' vanishing from view. In knowing the complete saga we see the saving transformation of each and every tragedy, no matter how great or small, in the stories concerning Jesus and, by corollary, concerning us.

This correlation is deceptively simple. We share the human nature of the Word made flesh. While Jesus was wholly God, Jesus was also wholly human. And it is the Lord's humanity, the Lord's movement from life to death, from sense to non-sense, which these meditations celebrate. The other amazing part of the story, of humanity becoming divine, is something we must await with faith and hope.

Seeing Is Believing

Many people have a favorite image of the crucifixion. It may be a subconscious image or one that is repeatedly renewed, through a painting, an icon or a personal object of devotion. These images often tell us a lot about ourselves. You may like a depiction which places Christ far away, on the hill outside the city of Jerusalem. As you look up you can see that something is happening up there, but you cannot quite see what it is. Or it may be something more gritty, almost vicious. Perhaps it is the portrayal of Jesus hanging as a dead weight, Jesus' crushed feet seeming larger than life, as painted by Grünewald in his *Crucifixion* on show in the public art gallery, the Kunsthalle, in the German city of Karlsruhe. Or you may like to take a more detached perspective. Perhaps you look from above, such as the hauntingly beautiful painting of the *Christ of St. John of the Cross* by Salvador Dali.

A Present-Day Image

There are many ways to look at the crucifixion. We are people looking at the scene from the distance of time and so we rely on images. Yet despite the passage of time, the images are constantly being renewed. There is one such image, a powerful one, in a recently constructed church in north London. It is one of many arresting features in the church of St. Paul's, Harringay.

It is a tall building with a steeply pitched roof. From the street you can clearly discern a glass triangle. When you look at the front of the church, the triangle appears to hover above the red-brick construction and its recessed doors. This effect is achieved by the roof's jutting out over the rest of the façade, along with a change in building materials. It all combines to give an imaginative illusion of the Trinity soaring above the surrounding area.

Inside, the design concentrates the attention on the main elements of the liturgy. Many things are highlighted by straight lines and a stark visual contrast. The main colors in the fabric of the building are black and white. A bold contrast is used for the liturgically necessary furnishings for the sacraments of Holy Communion and baptism. The altar and the font have been carved from a specially imported red stone.

There is also a feeling of soaring height within the building. This height directs the eye upward. There, on the wall behind the altar, is an extraordinary splash of color. Looking up at the wall you can make out the three crosses of the crucifixion. Continued inspection reveals that the crosses are not on the colored panels of the sculpture. They are actually in the gaps between them. The reredos is in thirteen sections. The spaces between the eight upper sections mark the outline of the three crosses of Golgotha.

It is a magnificent work of art. As you look up at it you feel you are being drawn through the cross. You are taken into it and beyond it. The surrounding panels give an extraordinary perspective. After a while you can forget you are on the ground looking upward. You can be taken over by another illusion. The illusion is that you are on the top of a hill looking down. You are looking down on a fractured landscape. Parts of it are discernible—names give us clues—but it moves from form and color to a brownish, unformed mass. You are looking down on the world. Then you are struck by a thought. You are standing *behind* the crucifixion.

With this perspective, Stephen Cox, the artist responsible for the reredos, altar and font, has fractured one of the more traditional impressions of the scene. He has turned the traditional rounded window shape for a reredos upside down. And within what he has done, the perspective is not the usual one, of us standing below Jesus Christ and looking up to the Lord hanging upon the cross. Instead, we are given a view of the world from the cross. We see the world from the perspective of the crucified Savior.

What the artist achieves is a transformation. We are taken from the passive to the active. The perspective shifts from the observer to the participant. Our point of view changes from the spectator to the spectacle. From our viewing we become the view. In our looking, we can see what lies beyond our look. We come to look through the eyes of the person we are observing. And from that sight, we can see.

This transformation is a stunning place to start. The reredos proclaims the simple complexity of the story of forgiveness extended for all people. In Jesus' death, brutal as it was, we can see Jesus' compassion for the world. This love and concern is typified in the lament Jesus made over the city for which he wept.

> *Jerusalem, Jerusalem, the city that kills the prophets and stones those who are sent to it! How often have I desired to gather your children together as a hen gathers her brood under her wings, and you were not willing! See, your house is left to you, desolate. For I tell you, you will not see me again until you say, "Blessed is the one who comes in the name of the Lord."* (Matthew 23:37-39)

In the reredos at St. Paul's, Harringay, we see not only the event. We are not restricted to Jesus' death on the cross. We also see its potency. We see that Christ's death is a once-for-all saving action. Through it forgiveness is extended. We see the effects it offers to all people. It places the crucifix at the center of time. Its power lies in the fact that, while it marks something which has already happened, the story has not ended. Its impact continues. The crucifixion includes not only those behind the cross but, because of the one who hangs upon it, it looks forward to others. It embraces the past and the future. It incorporates us.

It suggests shades of that old folk hymn:

> *Amazing grace! How sweet the sound*
> *That saved a wretch like me!*
> *I once was lost, but now am found,*

Was blind, but now I see.

(JOHN NEWTON 1725-1807)

The Twofold Element in the Passion

The reredos in St. Paul's, Harringay is a good starting point for a sensing of the Passion. It calls to mind that twofold element in the dramatic events which led up to the death of our Lord. There is what Jesus saw and what others saw. As we accompany Jesus from the Last Supper to death, we will concentrate on this dual understanding of the senses. We will look at the events of the Passion as experienced by Jesus. And we will look at the same events as experienced by the people who witnessed them: who saw them, who heard them, who smelled them, who touched them, who tasted them.

There is a real distinction between seeing and being seen. Think of an actor on a stage. The actor's view is on what is happening in front of her. She sees other people coming and going. She may be aware that there is an audience but we do not expect her to notice it. In naturalistic drama her concentration remains firmly within the depicted room on stage. An imaginary fourth wall, along the edge of the stage, contains the action. For the actor all the events occur inside the room. The convention of the absent fourth wall allows the audience to look on.

This focus of concentration is similar for a soccer player. To take too much notice of the spectators, to look and listen to their encouragement or derision, takes the player's mind off the game.

Indeed, many derisive comments have that desired effect. He takes his eye off the ball. If the player wants to win the ball, he must watch carefully. He must keep his attention on what is happening in front of him. He takes care to note where the ball is. He maintains a check on other players, on how and where they make their moves about the field.

In both cases, in the theater or the soccer stadium, what the audience sees can differ. To some extent we all see the same event. As one we watch the play or the game as it unfolds. We are caught up with it. There is a collective understanding of the plot of the play or the moves in the game. And yet, at the same time, we are each individual witnesses to these events. We each have a different perspective on them. Something said during the play may move us deeply because it affects something in our life or in our memory. The very same comment may leave the person sitting next to us completely unmoved. At the game we can be thrilled by a glancing kick which results in a goal. But for someone supporting the other side, it is to be dismissed as a mere fluke. Where you come from, who you are, what you have done, all affect your reactions to the scene.

Watching has all these disparate elements. That's why we use the term of someone having the "overall view." That idea, the overall view, is something which brings together many views. It combines the divergent perspectives of many people looking at one event or one person. It can take into account, in a positive or negative way, the placement, position and prejudice of the viewer.

This multilayered nature of events is just as true when we look from the opposite direction. For the actor or soccer player, it is a sole view of the surrounding world. And yet, in casting an eye across the audience or the crowd, his gaze can rest on one person. There can be intimate exchange, one to one, between the person taking part in the action and one of the many watching. It is a contrast in which the person in the center can see a corporate reaction or a solo one.

In the sensing of the Passion that solo view is Christ's. While looking out at the world, Christ's sight is also taking things in. Jesus' act of seeing is also the recipient of others' seeing of Jesus. Of one taking in many. In the reredos of St. Paul's, Harringay, Stephen Cox eggs us on to consider what may be the possible clash of these two views. We look at the conflict of the individual and the collective, and how that clash is continuing today.

While Jesus brings to the Passion the mind of God, our under-standing of it is through Jesus' human senses. That is because we share with the Christ human sensations. For both Christ and the viewer it is human sight which captures the action. We follow Christ from the table of the Last Supper, from the garden of Gethsemane, from the arrest and trial, from the walk to Golgotha, to Christ's death, knowing, all the while, that while it is all happening to God, it is done, seen and felt with the same senses that we have. It is done, seen and felt with human senses.

That is not to say our own faculties cannot be affected. Our senses can be affected by our emotions. They often are. A sense of panic can literally reduce our capacity of vision. The cliché that a person is so wound up about something that he or she cannot see the wider picture is true. When faced with a dilemma we are at risk of not seeing the events which have led up to it or which, indeed, may even be happening around it at the time. And the Passion is a very exciting, emotional time. The twofold aspect already mentioned, the crowd view and the solitary view, the Jesus view, are affected at various points by the emotions.

Indoors: The Last Supper

The first place one might see this is at the Last Supper. Again, think of a depiction of the scene you may have seen. People are looking at and to Jesus. Ostensibly they are there to celebrate the Passover, the traditional Jewish feast which takes place at that time of year. But by watching Jesus they can see, and are soon drawn into, a new event. Depending on the biblical account we read, we learn that they come to realize that this is the Last Supper.

It is also the first supper. It is the meal at which Jesus told the disciples to do as he did in his memory. The early church carried out the command of Jesus to reenact the meal. That command continues to be followed today in the celebration of the Eucharist. It is known by various names—Holy Communion, the Lord's Supper, the Mass. Whatever the name, it is a reenactment of that first supper which we know as the Last Supper.

This original supper in the upper room in Jerusalem comes

after an amazing sight. The first prophetic sign in the Passion narrative comes in a puzzling episode. Jesus had asked two of the followers to go on ahead, and Jesus told them what they would see.

> *"Listen," he said to them, "when you have entered the city, a man carrying a jar of water will meet you; follow him into the house he enters and say to the owner of house, 'The teacher asks you, "Where is the guest room, where I may eat the Passover with my disciples?"' He will show you a large room upstairs, already furnished. Make preparations for us there." So they went and found everything as he had told them; and they prepared the Passover meal.* (Luke 22:10-13)

This scene is one you may think you know well. But how have you come to that familiarity? It could be your remembrance of someone else's attempt to render the scene in visual terms. It may be the famous *Last Supper* by Leonardo da Vinci. Most paintings or sculptures of the event have a stagelike falsity about them. All the apostles sit on one side of the table. That way we can see all their faces. There are some marvelous pictures which alter the perspective. They take the view of the table from above. And what is actually on the table? For us, that can be something of a challenge. What was there? The commands in Exodus are fairly detailed, but it still requires our imagination to see it.

The meal was to follow the sacrifice of a year-old male lamb or kid, without blemish, its bones unbroken, slaughtered in the presence of the whole congregation of Israel at twilight on the fourteenth day of the month. It was to be roasted over a fire with its head and inner organs intact. It could not be eaten raw or boiled. And it was to be eaten with accompanying unleavened bread and bitter herbs.

And there were more instructions about how to eat it. Those at the feast would be dressed for an impending journey.

> *This is how you shall eat it: your loins girded, your sandals on your feet, and your staff in your hand; and you shall eat it hurriedly. It is the passover of the LORD.* (Exodus 12:11)

Foreigners could not take part. Anything left over had to be burned. And the story of this meal was to be kept alive. The Book of Exodus outlines a tradition maintained in Jewish households to this day. One of the children will ask the father of the house why all this is being done, and the story will be told again. But over time the custom has become adapted. In a progressive Jewish home today the celebration is stylized and evocative. It is a development from the instructions to the original actors in the Passover drama.

For us, at an even greater historical and social remove, the problems can be even more immense. How can we see Jesus and the disciples sitting at the table? Most renderings of the scene do have them sitting. Those on the periphery are sometimes standing, leaning in. Perhaps there is an appearance of relaxation, of contentment following a good meal. Or, depending on the moment the artist has chosen to depict, there is a range of reactions on the faces of the apostles. One is outrage at the suggestion of betrayal. Another is anger that one of their number is the traitor. There is bemusement, befuddlement and disbelief. Or there is sometimes even an appearance of pleasantly inebriated contentment on their faces. Concern has vanished. Whatever is to happen is beyond their control.

But the first and Last Supper has for Christians an added poignancy. It has more significance than the challenge in trying to picture how Jesus and the apostles would have arranged themselves around the table of the feast. It is also the night in which Jesus instituted our ongoing touchstone of Communion. It was the night Jesus gave us the assurance of the reality of God's presence among us. It is that which Christians celebrate every time in the Eucharist.

Let us look at this gift as the disciples did. We see Jesus take the bread, give the blessing and break it. Pieces of it fall to the table. We see the bread moving around. We watch it reducing in size as Jesus distributes it among them. We see Jesus take the cup, again give a blessing, and pass it round. We see the actions which accompany the command to do this in memory of the Christ. We watch Jesus' hands on the bread and the cup which he gives away, in the same way Jesus is to give away his life.

Watching someone else do something can be powerful. Often it is the gestures an individual used while speaking that we remember better than what he or she said. A habitual dabbing of the air while talking can have greater impact than an impressive argument. The gestures of someone inform many of us of the real attitude a speaker has to an idea. This is not necessarily expressed in words.

If you see a person hit his head there is almost an automatic emotional and physical response. It is a sympathetic feeling of the blow. You know just what that person is feeling. But the opposite is sometimes true. You witness an incident and cannot fathom the reaction a person is displaying. What he is doing does not fit in with your inner response to the incident. These are the times when you can see people and wonder, "Just what is all the fuss about?"

The Last Supper is full of that breadth of emotion. Each disciple necessarily sees a slightly different version of the same happening. They can be united in an overall statement of what broadly occurred. But that must come later. As the events unfold, each of them may have a particular insight because of a better view. His concentration may have been on one aspect of the proceedings. Something may have caught his attention and no one else's. One may have met Jesus' eye as Jesus passed the cup. There is the exchange of looks between their own number as the Lord speaks, as the gifts of the Lord's body and blood pass among them. One of them could catch sight of a falling crumb, of a spilled droplet of wine. One sees the bread moving round the table. Another looks at a succession of events: now at the face of the person accepting the gift, now at the bread and wine, the body and blood of the teacher.

And the man in the middle of the scene has the personal experience of being the focal point, but he witnesses some or all of others' individual insights. In that way it is right and proper to recognize Jesus as seeing the whole picture; of seeing Judas, either on the outer edge, as he is often depicted, or in the eyeball-to-eyeball contact that expressed so much when their hands were joined in the dish.

Did Judas look away? Or did he seek to brazen his way through? Could he meet the gaze of the person he had already decided to give over for thirty pieces of silver? There was a lot of looking around at the feast. The disciples looked at one another asking, "Is it I, Lord?" What were they looking for? Information? Confirmation that it was one of them? That among them was the traitor to whom Jesus referred?

The apostles' view takes in the progression of the meal. They see it move in its set order of presentation, through the consumption of the food to the stage of leftovers. At times, they notice that the tide-line of wine in cups and jugs has lowered. Every now and then they could have looked into their own cup and watched the hand as it moved to replenish the drink. In this they see themselves as part of what the ongoing Jewish tradition has laid out for them in the celebration of the Pasch, the Passover feast. Maybe they did realize the enormity of what Jesus was saying and doing. But did they show it? How was this knowledge to pass to onlookers, those at the feast, or to us who watch so long after that meal? How did they display their awareness that this supper was more than the continuance of the tradition, that it was a massive shift, a new beginning in which that supper would come to figure so prominently? By being there at the time and seeing it, they were part of the change.

The other, often neglected, part of this is what was happening outside the upper room. Was there a window? What was happening in the sky? Was it cloudy, clear? As the evening progressed did the room become dimmer, full of the foreboding we see in the exchange of glances? If the light was failing, did they have to lean in with more concentration, straining to see more clearly what was unfolding before their very eyes?

Outdoors: The Garden of Gethsemane

Let's move from the confines of the upper room. We are now in an open space. We look up, over and beyond buildings. There is a spring sky. The man-made environment has been replaced by a more natural locale. We are in the garden of Gethsemane.

People act differently outdoors. Think of the way people behave in public parks. Their movements are freer. They seem to relish a greater sense of space. This physical behavior can be an indication that inner constraints have been put aside. For the moment they are free from the concerns of home and work. Their cares have been left at the gate. They are experiencing a temporary release.

And yet in the midst of this liberating landscape, the disciples see a man getting tense. Jesus is getting worked up because he has not come to the garden to relax or to frolic about. Jesus has come to pray. And as the Lord does so we get those contrasting images between the Lord and the Lord's followers. Jesus is at one remove, alone, praying. Was Jesus' body rigid with the effort? Or was Jesus merely giving an impression of stress? Or perhaps Jesus' posture has some remnants of the jubilation expressed in John's farewell discourse? A traditional picture of this scene has Jesus kneeling, locked in concentration. And that image derives from the account of the Christ's praying so hard that sweat poured down like blood.

These are interesting sights. Yet there are doubts to be aired. If the three disciples were asleep while Jesus prayed, how could they see what was going on? Who was alert enough to report it? We must draw back from that. We see a broader picture of contrasts. We see Jesus awake and struggling while Jesus' friends are dead to the world. It is that contrast which is important. There is concentrated action and stillness. In Jesus is the realization of what is happening. Jesus knows what is to occur and the consequences. Jesus sees the consequences for the recumbent, sleeping disciples, and further. Jesus sees the moment and beyond it.

The Arrest

The arrival of the excited crowd is a stark change of scene: from the intimate gathering in the upper room, to the ironic closing down of perspective in the otherwise open setting of the garden. Into an open space comes a crowd. One of the perplexing things about crowds is their joint nature. They can be driven by a unitive force.

Yet while they can give the appearance of being as one, they are made up of many people.

So there is this approach of a corporate being, the crowd, with all the individual aspects it brings with it. There is enjoyment on someone's face, malice on another's. Some are bewildered. They show a questioning: "Just what is going on?" "What is this all about?" Each face has its own story. Each displays knowledge or ignorance of what is happening. There is the stern visage of someone in authority. The alert countenance of a guard shows an acceptance of this, just one of many unsavory tasks to be completed in the line of duty. Crowds also have ragged edges. There one can see movements of people trying to get a glimpse of the action. At the same time others push back, not so much to obliterate the view, but to mark some small measure of personal territory. There is also the excitement of those not in the vanguard pressing on from behind. This results in jostling. It leads to a ragged movement with many coming to a halt as the group finds its quarry.

This moment of the crowd's discovery of Jesus is one when we can see a united response. The message moves back through the ranks. The officials brace themselves for action. The onlookers galvanize themselves for the entertainment. The main players check themselves in the knowledge that what is to unfold is both private and on show for all to see.

The duality is found in a moment, in a piercing look as two people, Jesus and Judas, meet in the depths of eye-to-eye contact before the kiss. A glance which contained what? Pity? Steel-like resolve? Reluctance? Anger? Realization of the enormity of the action which expressed in the eye what Jesus said:

Judas, is it with a kiss that you are betraying the Son of Man? (Luke 22:48)

And there are the many sights of those watching this exchange. We see the crowd with its mixture of feelings. The disciples leap forward to exchange blows. Others try to hold back the enthusiasm and to stem the tide of violence. We glimpse a restraining arm here, a blocking grip there, pushing, shoving. All this color and movement, as theater choreographers call it. Hollywood epics tended to generalize this. The directors often choose to focus on the exchange between Jesus and Judas. For that they go in for the close-up. They avoid the crowd, using it more as a backdrop for the concentrated visual attention to the central action.

Yet both groups, those coming out to arrest Jesus and those in the garden with Jesus, have something to see and be seen. The difference is first in their numbers. A crowd meets a group. The second discrepancy is in equipment. We are told that the disciples had arms. They faced a crowd which had swords and clubs. Among its number were soldiers, professionally armed and trained. Despite this gap the disciples display the readiness to take up and use the little weaponry they have. One moves in to battle against the larger, more imposing adversary. And again, in the midst of all this movement and excitement is the discernible stillness of one person. Jesus gives a command which is seen to have immediate effect.

> *Put your sword back into its place; for all who take the sword*
> *will perish by the sword.* (Matthew 26:52)

After such a dramatic hiatus Jesus and Jesus' followers are absorbed into the crowd as the Lord is led off to the number of trials of which the Gospels give account. The Hollywood image again holds good here. Jesus is pinioned between soldiers. The Lord exudes a stillness in the face of the grim determination of the military carrying out their duty. Around Jesus can be seen the diverse reactions of the crowd moving as one from the garden. There are arms raised to accompany cheers. Scuffles break out within the crowd as they press on too quickly. Resentment is being expressed. Jesus' followers are abused as they are either absorbed into the crowd or as they fearfully quit the mob. Torches cut the night sky. Sparks seem to bounce off the spears. All these aspects are caught up in the movement behind the prisoner who, in true Hollywood style, stands serene and in his own special light.

The Panorama of the Trials of Jesus

The trial continues this panorama of contrasting views. But there is one contrast in which we can see the gaps between those who accuse and try Jesus, and the person on trial. In the synoptic Gospel accounts, Jesus is first brought before the Sanhedrin, the supreme Jewish council and the highest religious court. In this encounter we can see the crowd involved. We see the open mouths of cheering, of cries for mercy. Hands are raised in the urging on of those hearing evidence. There is movement to encourage the judges to condemn the person who stands before them for what he says. The crowd can see the enormity of the exchange. The blasphemous utterance of which Jesus is accused is so appalling to the high priest that he tears his clothes. This is a strong visual symbol to those looking on. They know the crime. The accused is then rocked by blows. For a while, blindfolded by his tormentors, Jesus cannot see the blows as they approach. But the crowd can see and it expresses its excitement in gestures of encouragement. There are also futile movements to hold back the hand of the attackers. In the end Jesus is bound, Jesus' movement curtailed even more tightly.

The visual contrasts continue when the trial moves to the Roman court. As soon as Jesus is brought in, it is clear that Jesus and Pilate have little in common. This is a scene in which the local confronts the imperial presence. The architecture of the palace is not indigenous; the dress, from haircut to robes, is that of a foreign power. This is seen again and again in the dress of the attendants, the military, the people who live within the palace. The chasm between them is often caught in religious art. The bearded peasant, dressed in a flowing robe, stands before the clean-shaven Roman in ceremonial dress. There is ordered restraint in the governor's presence and the formality of the proceedings as he tries to coax an answer out of Jesus. An abiding sight of this for me was captured in the Andrew Lloyd Webber/Tim Rice musical *Jesus Christ Superstar.* Pilate writhes as he tries to elicit some response. All the while Jesus stands stock still, physically expressing that simple statement of the gospel writer:

> *But he gave him no answer, not even to a single charge, so that*
> *the governor was greatly amazed.* (Matthew 27:14)

This scene is the starting point for the Stations of the Cross. The Stations of the Cross are, by and large, an imaginary exercise. They were invented and are used to explore the final hours of Jesus' life. They can lead to a focused meditation on some of the more graphic and gruesome aspects of the Passion. The first of the stations is of Jesus being condemned to death. It variously has Jesus in front of a musing Pilate, or has the governor washing his hands. That action informs us that, while Jesus is to die, Pilate believes Jesus to be guilty of no crime.

There is a filmic element in the tale at this point, a directorial change of vision. The action cuts to the moment Jesus is brought before the crowd. There is an explosion of fierce excitement. Again Jesus is guarded by the very people from whose number Jesus has been abused. The Lord is flanked by the soldiers who mocked and scourged him. Arms are thrashing and flailing to punctuate the crowd's demand for the freedom of Barabbas. All of this is taken in by the eyes of Jesus.

Some churches render dramatic readings of the Passion during Holy Week. The person reading the part of Christ can gain an insight into the loneliness of Jesus at this stage of the humiliating trial. In such readings one person gets to say the words that Jesus is reported to have said. We see a similar kind of substitution every time Holy Communion is celebrated. One can witness the responsibility of a priest while he consecrates the elements of bread and wine. The priest is the representative of the gathered community saying the words that Jesus said at the Last Supper. There is a hushed respect in the recreation of that event. But for a person taking the role of Jesus in the dramatic Passions, there is a powerful reminder that the condemnation of Jesus was made by ordinary people, by people of Jesus' own community.

Eric Franklin, an Oxford lecturer, used to make a point of this. "Don't think," he would say, "that Jesus was strung up by a rogue element. He was strung up by devout, God-fearing people. People for whom blasphemy was a serious crime. And, for them, Jesus was a blasphemer."

Jesus stood there, seeing the fervor in their faces. And among them Jesus saw some who had come along merely for the spectacle.

Watching the Walk to Calvary

Then there is the walk to Calvary. The British deaf community has a sign which captures the essence of eyes turning to look at an individual. The hands are splayed and the tips of the fingers are turned upward toward the face of the signer. The implicit eyes on the fingers are turning to the person in the middle. What a range of looks our Lord would have encountered! A mixture of excitement, enjoyment and compassion—because there must have been compassion in those who could not look and turned away.

From the perspective of Jesus there is an ever present view, the ground. Jesus looks down to avoid the hostility. Our Lord sees the earth as he bends under the weight of the cross. The ground comes closer each time as Jesus tries to absorb the weight. It presses down with every step in Jesus' attempts to battle on. Every now and then the Lord looks up, checking to see what lies ahead. Again Jesus sees the mixture of individual and corporate emotion that makes up a crowd. Jesus' vision is impaired as sweat drips into his eyes, then onto the ground below.

Then there are the close contacts, those ones, of biblical or pious tradition, captured in the Stations of the Cross. There is the longing look exchanged between Mary and Jesus in the fourth station. This captures a poignant moment as mother and child encounter each other on the road to Golgotha. Look becomes touch and look again in the apocryphal sixth station. What did Veronica see as she wiped the face of the battered Jesus? There is a confusion of glance and avoidance in the eighth station in which Jesus meets the women of Jerusalem. Their sight is dimmed through tears. Yet Jesus counsels clarity of vision.

Daughters of Jerusalem, do not weep for me, but weep for yourselves and for your children. (Luke 23:28)

When the journey ends, even more terrible sights are in store. The actual placing of Jesus on the cross is an event held in the eye of the crowd. They watch as the condemned person closes his eyes in pain and torture, and is hauled aloft.

Then there is the traditional sight of the Passion. Survivors do the looking. We stand in front, or slightly down the hill, as Jesus hangs upon the tree. Blood, sweat, spittle ooze from him. Sometimes Jesus is alone. Around Jesus can be different personages. Sometimes Jesus is with the others killed with him. Or Jesus is depicted with witnesses, Jesus' mother and John, Mary Magdalene, soldiers and Pharisees. They look up. Sometimes the sight is over-powering. In the *Crucifixion* from the Isenheim altar frontal, on display in Colmar in France, Mary swoons. John catches her as she falls. These scenes allow us to venerate and contemplate. We see the reality despite the romantic nature of many paintings of this death. But in our veneration we see ourselves as part of the story. As part of the event in which the sins of the world and those on it and in it—our sins—are laid to rest.

But there is an end to this sight. Those who watched the event saw a final slump in the broken body of the prisoner. They witnessed the signal to the world that all of Jesus' senses had ceased to function. They could see that the vision of Jesus had come to end. Jesus saw no more.

Jesus' eyes could have remained open, but Jesus' sight had failed.

Jesus' human sight is in darkness. Matthew's Gospel also tells of a cosmic darkness. This is portrayed in the earth shaking and the rocks splitting in two. The light is gone. Yet for those who come after there is a glimpse, a view ahead. They can see through the crucifixion to the future, as so marvelously captured by Stephen Cox in his reredos at St. Paul's, Harringay.

EXERCISES

1. Do you have a favorite picture of some part of the Passion? The crucifixion? On the road to Golgotha? The Last Supper? Try to see the painting in your mind's eye. If you are in a group you may want to show each other a copy of the picture. If you do not have a copy, try to explain what it looks like and how it affects you. Is there anything about it you would like to change? A color, a shade, a view?

2. Use the image you recall or find a picture of the Last Supper. Select one person from the painting—it could be Jesus or Judas—and try to see what is happening at the moment the artist has captured. Put yourself into his place. See what is on the table. Look at what is happening around you. Be careful to look to the edge of the picture. Is someone or something blocking your view? Try to enter that moment. See how you get around the obstacle. If you cannot, how do you keep yourself informed of what is going on?

3. Staying with the character, imagine that person:

- in the room;
- in the garden of Gethsemane;
- outside the trial of Jesus;
- at the crucifixion.

4. If you are meeting in a group, try to replace the faces of the apostles of the picture with the faces of the people in your group. Remember to keep yourself in the picture, but move others into that memory of the Last Supper.

5. If you could be in the crowd which follows the events, where would you see yourself? Where would you be most comfortable? Or where would you find it most unpleasant? At the center? In the front? In the midst? On the edges?

6. Sitting comfortably, place your hands on your lap. Close your eyes. Breathe in and out. Think of nothing but your own breath. Then concentrate on three colors—the color of the wall in the upper room, the color of the sky in the garden, and darkness of the clouds after the death of Jesus. Let the colors fade. Return your attention to your breath. Open your eyes again.

QUESTIONS FOR REFLECTION AND DISCUSSION

1. As human beings, we have a tendency to confine our spirituality to the head—thinking and talking rather than experiencing.

How can a study of the senses help to move us from the head to the heart, from information to Christian formation?

2. Even though God created us as a remarkable network of body, mind, and spirit, how do our churches neglect this unity? How can you help your church to honor this wholeness?

3. The author speaks of being able to see the world from the view of the cross. What insights to our daily lives do we gain by looking through the lens of Jesus?

4. As others observe our behavior as Christians, what do they see? When a visitor enters our church or Sunday school class, how do our gestures and body language communicate a welcoming atmosphere?

5. As Jesus was praying in the garden of Gethsemane, dealing with heartbreaking struggle, Jesus discovered the disciples sleeping. In what ways do we "sleep," detaching ourselves from those in the midst of painful experiences? Are we in denial ("sleeping") regarding our own pain? How can we be compassionately present with others and ourselves, truly *seeing,* rather than turning away?

6. How does your reflection on the Passion of Christ move you from sight to insight?

God, we give thanks for the gift of sight.
May we use it to see more clearly. Let us be joyful
for the many shades of light and color which it can discern.
May we remember that our view is one view.
Even when it becomes part of a broader picture,
let us recall it is never the complete, overall view.
We give thanks for the Savior, for Jesus' vision
of purpose and Jesus' compassionate sight on us.
May the power of your sustaining Spirit bring what we see
into the unifying vision of you in the Godhead.
We ask this through our Redeemer, Jesus Christ. Amen.

Blessed Are Those Who Hear

I want you to call to mind two kinds of sound. The first will be relatively easy for those people who live in towns or cities with a soccer stadium nearby. The other will be simpler for those who live in the country. Either way, one sound should be easier to recall than the other. That may take a little more concentration or imagination.

The first sound is the roar of the stadium crowd. If you did not know it already, the sheer noise informs you of something: that the local team is playing at home. Depending on how far you are from the stadium, the roar can have a compelling excitement. Those who live in such places will also know that there are different kinds of crowd roar. With a little exposure, you can come to discern the various messages being unwittingly communicated. You can tell what is happening on the field by the sound of the crowd. The cry that accompanies a near miss, perhaps a good shot interrupted by a vigilant goalkeeper, is very different from the derision which greets a lousy shot. You can hear if the crowd is happy or disappointed. It is possible to know if the spectators are united in the ragging of a player, or in their disagreement with a referee's decision. You can tell when they are bored. The chant "Why are we waiting?" is not a question. It is more a command that the game should get under way. Or, if play is already taking place, it is an expression of dissatisfaction. It is a call for a bit of action to be played out to meet the expectations of people in the stands.

The overheard noises can be interpreted. And there is one sound which is unmistakable. It does not need translation. It is the solid cheer, a clear clarion that a firm shot at goal has found its mark. There is an exultant roar of joy, of jubilation. And yet, on listening more closely, one can hear a more complex web of sounds within the cheer. This overwhelming acclamation is intermixed with moans and groans, the verbalized disappointment of the supporters of the team against whom the goal has been struck.

There is nothing secret about these sounds. Or the action upon which they are a commentary. The noise is an immediate reaction to what is occurring inside the stadium. It then travels to let others, not in the stadium, keep track of how the game is going.

The second sound is more intimate. It is almost a secret experience. It is the snapping of a twig underfoot in a forest. In a sheltered space, the crushing of a dead piece of wood can sound mighty. The simple snapping of a twig lets us know that our bulk has the power to destroy. Within the canopy of a wood, small noises seem to reverberate. We can find many reasons for this impending closeness of sound. The branches and leaves can filter out the noise which would normally reach our ears. There is a separation from the wider world. There is less competing noise around us. There are fewer people and cars. There is less industry. Whatever the reasons, an isolated snap can dominate because it seems to be amplified.

These two sounds and how they are communicated to us—the public roar and the intimate snap—are central to the Passion. In the

Passion narratives there is a lot to hear. There is a lot of conversation, questioning, roaring, cheering. During Holy Week, in many churches, the Passion of our Lord is either read alone or presented dramatically by a number of people. During those readings we hear a lot of talk. We hear it from Peter and the apostles. We hear it from the broader circle of disciples. We hear it from bystanders, from the crowd, from the high priests, from Pontius Pilate, from soldiers, passersby and mockers. And we hear it from Jesus.

What Jesus Says

The words and noises of these events, the precise way in which they were heard, differ in the gospel accounts of the final hours of Jesus. In the Gospel of John Jesus talks a great deal. Jesus certainly speaks a great deal more about himself than in the record of any of the other evangelists. But then the proclamation of John is a proclamation of Jesus' self-knowledge. Several times during the Last Supper, Jesus reiterates the point made several times in John's account of Jesus' ministry and life. Jesus points out the significance of himself, as borne out in his relationship to the source of all being.

> *Very truly, I tell you, the hour is coming, and is now here, when the dead will hear the voice of the Son of God, and those who hear will live. For just as the Father has life in himself, so he has granted the Son also to have life in himself; and he has given him authority to execute judgment, because he is the*

Son of Man. Do not be astonished at this; for the hour is com-
ing when all who are in their graves will hear his voice and
will come out—those who have done good, to the resurrection
of life, and those who have done evil, to the resurrection of
condemnation. I can do nothing on my own. As I hear, I judge;
and my judgment is just, because I seek to do not my own will
but the will of him who sent me. (John 5:25-30)

John uses the farewell discourse at the Last Supper to stress this vital link between the Father and the Son. For that reason, perhaps, as well as its sheer length, the dramatic rendering of the Passion of John tends to start well after the Last Supper. Yet to ignore those words is to ignore the ultimate message of the triumph of life over death.

Actions and Explanations

In the Passion of John we are given clues to make sense of what is to follow. Before we hear the words there is a startling sound. We hear the splashing of water. There is the scraping of a bowl on the floor as Jesus moves from disciple to disciple. Then comes the slosh of water and the rubbing of hands and cloth on feet as Jesus washes and dries their feet. After hearing the action, we hear the explanation. Christians are to live an inverted life. They may not be very good at it, but they are told to live a life which topples the established order. Jesus explains the purpose behind the noises.

You call me Teacher and Lord—and you are right, for that is what I am. So if I, your Lord and Teacher, have washed your feet, you also ought to wash one another's feet. For I have set you an example, that you should do as I have done to you.
(John 13:13-15)

Jesus then goes on into what is known as the farewell discourse. Films tend to capture this in a concentrated stillness. The apostles lean in, hanging on every word that Jesus speaks. But they were having dinner. Perhaps the clatter of bowls, cups and food was an accompaniment to the important words being said. There is no snub in this. Every dinner party has a certain subconversational symphony. Hospitality and enjoyment are expressed openly through discussion, but also in the sounds of knife, fork and plate. Or in a glass being filled with wine. At the first and Last Supper we can hear the passing of food and drink, polite tapping on others' clothing to pass this or that. Yet the guest of honor, the person who has led the disciples there, says something which brings a devoted concentration. The noise level drops for a moment to silence.

Jesus says he is going to be betrayed. There is an intake of breath. And the momentary stillness is cut asunder. Muttering starts. Muted conversation bubbles away. The apostles try to tease out the significance of what the Lord has said. Does Jesus really mean this? Is it another clever saying we have missed the point of? Is the betrayer truly one of us? Which one? Such confusion is not totally verbal.

Seating is scraped across the floor. There is a bump on the table. There is an audible rustling of clothes. Mounting tension brings silence to an end.

Jesus confirms that the traitor is one of their number. This revelation leads to a clatter. A seat is drawn back. There are footsteps across the floor. A door is opened and for a moment sounds of the outside world filter in. In a flash, it is obvious that this essentially private scene is taking place in a larger world. The concerns of others are real and can affect something as private and intimate as this dinner. The door closes and Jesus begins to talk. The Lord starts to explain to the disciples what is about to happen and what its significance is.

Jesus tells them he is to be glorified. Again, Jesus' attempt to speak is halted. Peter interrupts. This time he wants to tag along. The Lord tells him it cannot be done. Peter protests. And Jesus tells him that another sound will confirm what he has said. It will be the crowing of the cock, when Peter will recognize the truth in the prediction that he will deny all knowledge of his Master.

Jesus then takes up the discourse again. Jesus stresses his link to the Father. Jesus says that a fullness of understanding, impossible at this time, will come in the form of the Counselor, the Spirit of truth. They hear a promise of care, of inspiration. The church today celebrates the fulfillment of that promise in the celebration meal of Holy Communion.

The Last Supper is also the time we hear the words which are repeated, in various forms, each time the Eucharist is celebrated.

The disciples hear their Lord and Master declare that he will not eat the Passover meal again until it is fulfilled in the kingdom of God.

> *While they were eating, Jesus took a loaf of bread, and after blessing it he broke it, gave it to the disciples, and said, "Take, eat; this is my body." Then he took a cup, and after giving thanks he gave it to them, saying, "Drink from it, all of you; for this is my blood of the covenant, which is poured out for many for the forgiveness of sins." (Matthew 26:26-28)*

It was not just the words which could be heard. Actions were audible. There is a rustle of clothing as the cup is passed from one disciple to another. There is the occasional slurp as, in a mixture of awe, confusion and perhaps even embarrassment, someone realized the enormity of what has been said. Can it be true? Did Jesus really mean that? For Jews to drink blood is sin. The Law declares that in blood is the life of an animal. For that reason the food strictures ensure that blood is drained or cooked off. Meat is not to be eaten raw. And here is Jesus, not only telling them that what is in the cup is Jesus' blood, Jesus' life, but that they must drink it. Perhaps one of the disciples balks at this injunction. He is not able to comprehend what Jesus has asked him to do with the Law. His hesitancy brings a grunt or words of encouragement from those around him. They share the confusion, but believe Jesus will reveal what he means by the words.

As the cup is being passed round, the words of Jesus echo again, and they hear the bread being broken. This large, tearing sound can have a number of small echoes. Crumbs hit the plate and cloth, each giving a separate resonance to the action. The sound of chewing starts and increases as the bread is passed from one to another. This personal noise of mastication reduces the awareness of external sounds.

Sounds in the Garden

Let us leave the upper room and fill our ears with a different sound. Radio dramas are often played out against a background of what their producers call ambient sound. The noise of a factory, for instance, will be taped. It gives the atmosphere of being inside. The clashes and clangs tell us where we are in relation to the machines. The action portrayed by the actors occurs in the midst of this noise. It dictates how they say the words scripted for them. By changing this ambient sound the listener knows that the action has moved in time or place, say from the factory to somewhere outdoors. Not only does the ambience change but the actors too must alter their sound in relation to it.

We do not speak the same way when we are indoors as when we are outdoors. So much of our behavior depends on what is happening around us. In the woods people tend to lower their voices, as if in respect for the existing quiet around them. If we are in a room where a television or radio is blaring away loudly, we have to speak up to be heard. The same goes when we are outdoors. We do not speak or hear in the same way when we are on the corner of a busy intersection as we would in a quiet park.

The ambient sound in the second stage of the Passion is one of open space and quiet. Sounds of the town drift up to the garden but they are subdued, reverential, in tune with the Passover celebrations. There is a breeze in the branches of trees. There is a rustle in the leaves around us. And through this we hear a clamor. We detect an indication that the relative calm of the moment is going to be changed.

It is the sound of an approaching crowd. Try to imagine this crowd of people. Who makes it up? What kind of people are they? Each of us has a particular sound. We each have a personal noise. We call it our voice. But there are some sounds we have in common. It may be our dialect. The way we speak can alert a hearer as to where we come from. What we say identifies us. It may also be in our use of certain words or phrases.

This crowd has that range of sounds. Into the general ambience of the garden comes the twofold nature of a crowd. There is a corporate noise. It is a unified sound yet is made up of many divergent utterances. As the crowd approaches we can hear these differences of tone, timbre and pitch. There are aural codes to identify the people who make them. There is the formal, almost legalistic, speech of the more educated. They have been sent along to superintend what is about to happen. They will make sure it happens and they do so efficiently, without actually being involved in the action. There is the commanding voice of the leader of the soldiers. The ranks respond with military sharpness. We hear regimented walking in time. Feet hit the ground in well-trained measure. There is a clink of equipment as the soldiers move forward. And behind the soldiers, in and among all this, there is the excited mixture of cries. There are voices of the highborn and lowborn, the local and foreigner, the young and old who have come along to witness the event.

This kind of entertainment involves even the reluctant participant. Some know what it is all about and others are in the process of finding out. They ask the people around them. They try to find someone who can make sense of their language, their dialect, their accent. Some are content to make the journey, satisfied that the precise nature of the expedition will be revealed in time. Some may not even care or desire to know.

But independent of the makeup of the crowd, its approach would be heard. This is a different quality to the assumed tranquility of the garden. We can hear excitement in the roar of the crowd when it eventually finds Jesus. There is an opposition of sounds here. The crowd, like that in the soccer stadium, is encouraging the participants on but is also keen to hear the exchange of words between them. What they say will be worth remembering and telling others. What is said, heard and remembered makes a story. That too can be said and remembered countless times.

A hush falls upon them. Some are quiet because they are interested in what is happening. Others are stunned into silence. Because what they hear from the mouth of Jesus is the name of God. This utterance shocks. It is hard to express the enormity of this in

an age when "God" and "Jesus Christ" are routinely used as excla-
mations or curses. It takes some surfing across the cultural internet
to arrive at a place where utterance of the name of God is a con-
versation-stopper. This is especially so when it is used as Jesus used
it, in the comparatively simple phrase of identification: "I am he"—
the same words as the I AM by which Israel's God announced himself to Moses (Exodus 3:14).

The words are followed by a stunned silence. And then noise
breaks out in abundance. There is the sound of retreat. Body col-
lides with body. Feet shuffle on earth. Equipment is displaced.
There is mumbling, dissension, discussion with one another. Then,
like the soundtrack of an old swashbuckling movie, comes the
swish of swooping swords.

A cry of pain ensues. There are shrieks of fear that the violence
may engulf them all. Individuals voice anxiety that they may be singled
out in the clash of panic against order as the soldiers try to restore
order. They seek to retain their military calm. At the same time they
want to ensure that the wanted man is taken prisoner by an accredited
official. There are cries of disgust, calls for the blasphemer to meet his
end here and now. Again the confused and the foreigner cry out in
inquiry, only to be responded to in a string of noises which make no
sense to them. The crescendo of outrage and argument has its conclu-
sion in the authoritative command of Jesus to put the sword away.

This brings but a temporary lull. Again, there is a mixture of
noises from the crowd. There is a clamor from those who want

action and want it now. There are the calming sounds of those urging caution. And their words have a physical expression. It can be heard in the robust mixture of walks, the dragging of feet, the hobbling, in the determined march and the tentative step.

Crowds have two identities: the corporate and the individual. Just as we hear the united cheer from the soccer stadium, we know it depends on the individuals who make up the mighty roar. That almost obvious aspect is what rings out as Jesus is confronted. Having agreed to go with them, we hear the arguments and the cacophony of the physical as the crowd moves on its way to the next encounters in the Passion.

The Trials

It is worth pausing at the two trials of Jesus to take account of the diverse nature of the sounds being made and the way they are being comprehended. Much of aural communication depends on proximity. If you sit near the action, you can follow the intricacies of conversation. The further away you are, the more you rely on other sources of information. These might be what you can see, or what others tell you, or how you interpret people's reactions to events. And there is gossip. There is the ongoing press and murmur among the crowds. They trail behind the leading players, trying to hear the exchanges between the priests and Jesus. The report is necessarily garbled. Despite the individual reactions to what is heard, there are times when the crowd does unite in a roar. It is a singular demand for action. This commentary on the action is real but inescapably remote. For Jesus and Jesus' judicial adversaries, it is a reminder that this case is of major public concern.

There is no place where this is more evident than in the exchanges in which Jesus is asked to confirm that he is the Son of God, the Christ. The people around Jesus have official ears. They hear through the filter of their common understanding of the Law. They hear blasphemy when it is uttered. And Jesus responds to them that if he were to tell them he was the Son of God, they would not believe him. There are mutterings among them as they try to work out what question to put next. Whispered discussion centers on how they should understand what has been said already. They want to decide on what course the inquisition should follow. It is unlikely this was without dispute. But there is a person in authority, the high priest, who commands by his voice that the questions should be apt and managed through him.

There are other sounds besides the voices of the council of priests. There is the crack of an open hand across a face. There is the awful thud of fists into flesh as Jesus is beaten. The crowd hears the slap slightly after it sees it. But for Jesus the noise is near. It echoes in Jesus' ears and through Jesus' bones. Jesus groans as the air is forcibly expelled from his lungs. Those standing closest can hear Jesus gasp to recover his breath. This is followed by short catches of breath as Jesus steadies himself. Jesus wonders what he has done to deserve such treatment.

If I have spoken wrongly, testify to the wrong. But if I have spoken rightly, why do you strike me? (John 18:23)

As a response to this query, there is the violent sound of spit being projected and finding its target on the face of this person who is already pinned in torture. Those maltreating Jesus add to their abuse by taunting him in his pain, insisting that Jesus prophesy, and tell them who it was who hit him.

After these words comes an action which has its own sounds. There is a grating as rope is tied together. This is muted as the cords catch on clothing, only to be followed by a light hiss as they cut into flesh. Again these noises have a special intimacy for the person on whom the rope is being tightened. There is the grunt of those securing the prisoner and after the scuffling noises, the ambience changes to the open air. The crowd rejoices in the now undisputed prisoner. Taunts come to the ears of Jesus. A kaleidoscope of sounds starts again as the procession starts off. It is headed up by the clink and tap of military precision. There follows a shuffling to a place of even clearer contrasts. The destination is the praetorium and the trial before Pontius Pilate.

In many paintings of this scene, the crowd is kept far from the court. This puts their cheers and cries a way off. It allows us to listen carefully to the exchange of words between Jesus and the Roman governor. The Roman occupiers built things in a style different from that of the indigenous culture. Most occupiers do. They re-create a little piece of home, to give them some familiar comforts and to remind the locals that they are subject to a foreign power. The clearest message of the distinctive nature of occupiers can be heard. It is language. More often than not, in the history of imperialism, occupiers use their own language. The dominant power insists that negotiations between its representatives and the local populations are conducted in the foreign state's language.

In Jerusalem the language would have been Latin. Here is one of the great puzzles of the Gospels. If Pontius Pilate was an occupying Roman, what language was the interview conducted in? Did he know enough Aramaic to inquire of Jesus the matters he put to him? Was there an interpreter? Or did his accent present such a chasm to understanding that Jesus just did not know what was being asked of him? Is this the reason that Pilate's questions were met with silence?

This conversation between Pilate and Jesus, while of public interest, is a more private affair than that at the house of the high priest. Pilate is listening for some substance in what has been presented to him as an open-and-shut case. He wants to hear how the alleged offense to the local population fits into the legal system he is charged to administer. A suspicion that he is being asked to determine a matter outside his jurisdiction affects his hearing. He listens for information behind the words coming to his ears.

The exchange is edged with formality. Justice must not only be done but be heard to be done. And yet this formality is tinged with voiced exasperation. Words have an added meaning. They can be enhanced by tone, speed, stress and loudness. The judge must weigh the excited interruptions and urgings of his accusers. He listens to the repeated calls of those who want to see Jesus dead. In their turn, they listen not only to what Pilate has to say, but how he says it. The reply he gets to the question as to what offense Jesus has committed brings a straightforward but puzzling response. They tell Pilate that if Jesus were not an evildoer, he would not have been brought before the authorities.

Away from the accusers, Pilate attempts to break through the shell of Jesus. He assures Jesus that his foreignness is not to be feared but trusted. He asks Jesus what he has done, only to get the response:

> *My kingdom is not from this world. If my kingdom were from this world, my followers would be fighting to keep me from being handed over to the Jews.* (John 18:36)

The ruler hears. But does he choose to ignore the claim that the followers of the person before him are subversive? Does he understand that they will have to be different to the prevailing culture? After this there is the measured sound of footsteps across the hall. There is a change in the atmospheric noise as the judge goes on his own to meet the accusers. They have come with a predetermined judgment: death. Pilate tells them quite simply that he can find no crime in Jesus. Breath is drawn in. Disapproval is barked. Disbelief is snarled. Muttering starts about what next can be done to secure the condemnation of Jesus. Above the hubbub, the leaders make arguments to support their case.

There is a hush as Pilate proceeds with his ploy to counter the machinations of the elders. He goes over their heads and speaks to the crowd itself. People shuffle. Calls for order signify that the governor has something important to say. And it is a shock. He suggests Jesus should be released as a Passover gift. The crowd unites in a demand not for the release of Jesus but of a robber, Barabbas.

The synoptic Gospels also direct us to listen for a choruslike chant. The crowd, like a choir behind the judicial and priestly soloists, makes a united cry. It is a cry that uses one word, "Crucify!" Each voice, with its personal timbre, adds an edge to the sound which has one meaning: "Put this man to death."

Heard on the Way of the Cross

From here on words cease to be of overriding importance. The sounds of the Passion capture the torments of Jesus as he walks the road to Golgotha. At times Jesus is lost in the tumult of noise as he is grabbed and jostled. The tortuous cacophony continues in the ringing slaps to Jesus' face and thuds on Jesus' torso as he is manhandled. Jesus' body becomes an echo chamber to the actions being played out upon it. The crowd responds with excited cheering. Onlookers exchange oaths and insults. The crowd jeers at its victim, ignoring the stern rebukes of the supervising guards.

Jesus would hear all this but through a personal filter of his own noise as he struggles with the cross on his shoulders. There is a hiss as incoming breath is caught up with sweat and mucus. Jesus' knees crack as he falls to the ground under the instrument of his own death. Each fall brings quiet murmurs of encouragement, taunts of derision, cries of abuse from the crowd. It continues its various comments in the one word it cried earlier, "Crucify!"

It is not only the sounds of antagonism Jesus hears. Sympathy has its own aural expression. When Jesus is eased of the burden of the cross, his ears are freed to hear the surrounding cacophony. And in that cacophony there are the sounds of a man struggling with the weight of which Jesus has been relieved. Some sounds have a double meaning. To hear the noise of another person's accident communicates immediately the pain involved. Jesus hears in a different way the oblique crack of his knees on the road as he falls, unable to bear the weight of the cross. Jesus hears the bubbling of sympathy from those around him, those who understand what Jesus must be feeling. Jesus also hears cries of the women of Jerusalem, for whom he urges these noises be directed elsewhere:

Daughters of Jerusalem, do not weep for me, but weep for yourselves and for your children. For the days are surely coming when they will say, "Blessed are the barren, and the wombs that never bore, and the breasts that never nursed." Then they will begin to say to the mountains, "Fall on us";

and to the hills, "Cover us." For if they do this when the wood
is green, what will happen when it is dry? (Luke 23:28-31)

Our Lord hears another woman's sobbing. This time it is more
intense. It is smaller, more personal. Jesus hears a cloth being wiped
across his face. Its scraping is momentarily intensified as it brushes
past his earlobes. Veronica has removed the accumulation of sweat,
blood, tears and mucus from Jesus' face. Each of these bodily fluids
has a different texture and, because of that, each has a different pitch
as cloth is drawn across Jesus' face. This is refreshing as the barriers
to sound are removed in her caring gesture. But our Lord's refreshment is only fleeting as it prepares him for the clearer calls as people
in the crowd cry, exultant, sad or bewildered, as Jesus moves closer
to Golgotha and death. These cries subside, not because the crowd
has lost interest, but because of a cordon placed round the place of
execution. Only those particularly involved can get near. Jesus hears
the barking command of the soldiers telling the people to get back,
clear a way, allow those whose job it is to carry out the death sentence to get on with it.

Jesus' arrival is greeted with a mixture of cries of relief by those
waiting to carry out the execution. Theirs is a job of specific skills and,
as such, with specific accompanying sounds. A workmanlike removal
of clothes gives slight ripping noises. Then there is a punishing sound:
the thwack of wood on wood, then the clink of hammer on nail,
muffled as the metallic clink is absorbed, hushed by flesh, a crack of

bone and flesh, then the thud as it reports that the nail has hit wood. And through all this a cry, a series of piercing shrieks of pain. Watching a person in pain brings automatic reactions, sometimes in sighs of sympathy, other times in taunts of mock encouragement and enjoyment of someone else's suffering. The crowd would have both these vocal expressions.

Film representations often capture the range: the jeering crowd, the sneering remarks of the guards, the irony of one thief telling him to free himself from this torture, the second thief admonishing the criminal, Jesus' promise that this day he will join Jesus in paradise. Then words which tell us the end is near:

My God, my God, why have you forsaken me? (Matthew 27:46)

This causes the crowd to mutter. They ask themselves whether a marvel of deliverance is to be seen and heard. We hear the loud cry mentioned by Mark and Matthew, a cry in which Luke gives us the echo of Psalm 31:5:

Father, into your hands I commend my spirit. (Luke 23:46)

Or, the more triumphant:

It is finished. (John 19:30)

But there is also a personal soundtrack which does not involve words, as Jesus struggles with his brutal end. Through and amidst any speech are Jesus' reactions to pain. These are communicated in crying, gasps of discomfort and grief. They are made known in choking, stifling, awful cries of anguish. It is through this all too personally created ambience that our Lord would hear the calls of the crowd. The people looking on no longer make a united voice. They are now single voices which, despite whatever else is going on, must make their mark. And the end comes in a cry—or is it a gasp?—as Jesus says his last and nothing more is heard.

EXERCISES

1. Keep quiet for five minutes. This can seem a longer and more difficult task than you might think! Set an alarm clock which will sound at the end of the five minutes. That way you will not worry about how long it is taking.

• Listen to the noises around you. Those sounds nearer you—your own breath, the rustle of your clothes on furniture—take note of them. Do not try to engineer any sounds. Try to avoid making them. Just listen.

• Move the focus of your hearing to the sounds further away. The noises of people around you, the sounds outside the room, in other parts of the house, the street. Just listen.

• When the alarm rings, if in a group, discuss the experience of sitting together in silence. Was it comfortable? Was there anything which made the experience unhappy or disturbing? Share as much or as little as people want.

2. Again sit in quiet. Focus on the following sounds. If you are meeting in a group, having achieved quiet, ask members to listen to these three sounds from the Passion. Remember to set out what you will need beforehand.

- Pour water into a bowl. If in a group, get one of them to wash their hands as it falls.

- Get each member to wipe his or her face with a towel. Concentrate on the noise as the towel moves across your ears.

- Drive a nail into a piece of wood with a hammer.

3. Again sit quietly. Slowly read aloud Psalm 130.

QUESTIONS FOR REFLECTION AND DISCUSSION

1. Reflect for a moment on the power of sound in your everyday life—a train whistle, a child's cry, the wind in pine trees, the clamor of an athletic event. Try to identify the emotions that are aroused by these noises.

2. Still focusing on ordinary sounds that are a part of your life, name a sound that brings immediate joy to you. What sound stirs your compassion? Engenders serenity? Produces anger or impatience?

3. It has been said that "the silence of prayerful meditation is not the silence of the graveyard, but the silence of a garden growing." How does silence make us available to God's growth process for us?

4. Read the experience of Elijah's attempt to hear the voice of God as recorded in 1 Kings 19:11-13. In what circumstance did he finally hear God's guidance?

5. What keeps us from hearing "the still, small voice" of God? What other sounds obscure the divine voice?

6. How does God's voice come to us through liturgy? Sermons? Other corporate worship experiences?

Lord God, you have promised to hear the prayers of those who call on you. May we also hear your call. Let us listen to those who call on us. May their cries for help, understanding or assistance be heard in our minds and hearts. We give thanks for the sounds around us— the singing of the birds, the joys of music and the delight of speech. May we also cherish and give to others that gift of silence, a gift in which you also speak to those who listen. May we hear the words of our Savior, Jesus Christ, and may we make joyful sounds to proclaim Jesus' message of love, repentance and forgiveness. We ask you to hear our prayer through Jesus Christ our Lord. Amen.

An Odor Pleasing to the Lord

The Passion of Jesus Christ is rightly seen as an inversion of tragedy to triumph. This is in keeping with the teaching and actions of Christ. Jesus called people from what they were doing to something new and exciting. Jesus told them to follow him. Jesus challenged the accepted values of the people with whom he lived. Jesus was a leader who served. These were subversive acts. This subversion is continued in much Christian understanding about the death of Jesus.

Much of this understanding stems from a knowledge of the whole story. We know what happens before, during and after the Passion. We are in a position to understand what transpired because of it. We can see that the Passion is more than just a part of the final stages of the story of the life of Christ. Jesus' death is cherished not because of the brutality involved but because of what happened through it and what occurred after it. Christians see the death of Jesus as important because through it they claim the possible release from their sins. They also know that the execution of Jesus is powerful because of the resurrection. Christ's death becomes a victory. Through the resurrection and through the doctrine of atonement we have a transfigured failure.

This smell of success is, however, something we can savor only after the event. In retracing the Passion through the sense of smell, we must realize from the outset that these final hours are imbued with an odor of decay. We sense how the aroma of the Passion moves from the enticing smells of life to the stench of death. This is a very human progression. And yet it is tinged with a special piquancy because of our attachment to it. These often repugnant odors are altered to something pleasant because of what we know.

Part of this is because of an awareness that comes with age. Once we reach a certain age our bodies inform us that we are slowing down. Although it varies from individual to individual, we cannot avoid physical reminders that we are getting older. We can do much, through a healthy diet, exercise and the like, to be at our best. But we cannot halt altogether the progression of age. It is a human given. Compared with other animals, humans start at birth at an early stage of development. From that they move to maturity. It is not too long before the body commences a physical decline. In this progression we can be reminded of the challenge of faith.

> *Listen, I tell you a mystery! We will not all die, but we will all be changed, in a moment, in the twinkling of an eye, at the last trumpet. For the trumpet will sound, and the dead will be raised imperishable, and we will be changed. For this perishable body must put on imperishability, and this mortal body must put on immortality.* (1 Corinthians 15:51-53)

Once I met a man who explained to me the difficulty of trying to market perishable foods. He said the challenge of effectively selling such food lies in its very nature. The examples he cited were bread and butter. As soon as the product was made it had started the process of going stale. You could slow it down, perhaps, but nothing could stop it. He said it was fairly easy to discern when the goods had aged too far. You could smell it. This is true of many staples. Milk, for instance, has an odor when it is rancid.

The Passion of our Lord follows a similar pattern. In tracing the events of Jesus' last hours on earth we move from the experience of the sweet to the sour.

The Aroma of Two Meals

Let us draw first on the relatively familiar images of the Last Supper. One should expect the feast would have included those observances as laid down by the Jewish scriptures. Tradition has, in fact, enshrined two feasts. The first is sparse, symbolic, liturgical. It is purely religious. The second is more recognizable as a meal. It still celebrated the Passover but is more attuned to the needs and tastes of the diners. The celebration meal consists of foods prepared in accordance with food laws. But it is separate from what is known as the *seder,* the ordered meal.

The Book of Exodus has detailed instruction about how to prepare a household for seven days of unleavened bread. Eating even a small particle of leaven is against the Law. In many Jewish homes this practice still continues. Any rising agent which might be in the larder is thrown out to ensure the purity of the home. Only unleavened bread shall be eaten for seven days. There is a ritualistic and real search of the home which has a symbolic and practical effect of turning the household into the sanctuary. The house is cleared to make it ready for the time when people will gather around the table and recite the *Haggadah,* the text which incorporates the story and interpretation of the exodus of the chosen people out of slavery in Egypt.

The *seder* meal thus prepared has echoes of the twelfth chapter of Exodus. Here scripture tells of a feast of unleavened bread. The blood of the lamb is spread on the lintel of the doorposts to signify to the angel of death that this is a protected house. For that reason, to this day, the Passover meal has an air tinged with aroma. There are the smells of the two meals, the symbolic and the subsequent celebrational meal.

The *seder* table is laid out with special requirements. There is the *seder* plate on which is found foods through which the redemption story can be told. There is the *zeroah*, a shank bone of a lamb. This serves to remind those gathered around the table of the lamb offered at the original Passover. There is a roasted or hard-boiled egg, *beytza*, recalling the roasted egg offered at the temple of Jerusalem at the Passover festival. *Maror*, the bitter herb, usually horseradish or another strong vegetable or herb, alerts participants to the bitterness and hardship of slavery. *Haroset*, a salad consisting of a mixture of finely chopped apples, nuts, cinnamon and wine, serves to remind them of the mortar used by the slaves of Egypt. *Karpas*, parsley or celery, is on the *seder* plate as an indication of thanks to God for the goodness of the earth. This is a reminder of spring, the time of the Passover.

Also on the table is saltwater, a symbol of the bitterness endured by Israel in its slavery in Egypt. The *karpas* of the *seder* plate is dipped into the water. There is a separate plate on which is *matzot*, three pieces of unleavened bread, a reminder, among other things, of the patriarchs Abraham, Isaac and Jacob. Each person is expected to drink four cups of wine or grape juice. These four drinks, recalling the blood which the Hebrews sprinkled on the doorpost for the Passover, echo the four stages by which Israel was released from slavery. They were freed, delivered, redeemed and taken. One last cup remains. It is the cup of Elijah, an expression of deliverance, a symbol of the prophetic hope of the coming of the kingdom of God on his creation.

This is an important background to the Last Supper. Christians cherish the gathering in the upper room for the institution of Holy Communion. But even before Jesus commanded the apostles to continue the celebration, the meal was special. It was a special meal in Jewish custom. The disciples had gathered to celebrate Passover. It was Jesus who changed the significance of the feast, in the same way Jesus had changed the way they went about their lives. This meal then is tinged with a special odor.

Food has not only taste but smell. The two senses are closely linked. The combination of the fragrances of specially prepared meat, fruits and herbs would alert all those coming into the upper room that the *seder* meal was laid out. They would recognize odors of the ceremonial food. And they would gain a foretaste of the celebrational meal to come later. Each apostle has a personal reaction. They share our predilections when it comes to eating.

It is that second meal that teases the senses of the apostles. Fragrances can stimulate saliva and stomach juices. The apostles savor the smell of favorite foods, knowing their consumption is not long off. We do not know for sure what was on the menu. Paintings often depict it as a repast of some opulence. It would be safe to assume that the tang of spices, olives and fresh vegetables rose from the table. Seeing and smelling this fare is part of the delayed enjoyment of the meal. What food was the strongest to the nose?

The smell of a meal is often dominated by one part of it. A roasted leg of lamb can disguise the vegetables which have been cooked to accompany the flesh. Likewise aromas outside eating places can tell us what sort of food is available without the specifics being revealed. If you walk around a restaurant area of a town on a cold night it is possible to gauge what is being offered nearby by the smells in the air. You know when you are approaching an Indian restaurant. You cannot tell just which curry is being served but there is a general tandoori aroma.

The apostles are brought up short from their enjoyment. Jesus concentrates their attention on two parts of the meal, wine and bread. Having blessed it, Jesus passes the cup. Did the apostles pause to take a sniff? Were they bold enough to smell its contents to check if it was indeed blood? Anyone who has watched a program on television about wine will recognize the importance of the "nose" of the drink being savored. Here it is not the mere "nose" of the wine, but a key to the mystery of the Master's words which is being sought. Does wine smell like blood? The bread would smell of bread. What did Jesus mean when he said it was his body?

This continues in the obeyed command that Christians reenact in the new celebrational meal enshrined in the Last Supper. Holy Communion is a time when we, as modern-day disciples, share in the body and blood of Jesus. Many Christians share the puzzlement of the apostles. The body and blood smells like bread and wine. Yet the sacrament of the Eucharist is the place where the church maintains people can encounter Jesus in a real way.

Gethsemane: Garden Fragrance and the Smell of Fear

After the comparatively cooped-up, special-banquet smell, Jesus and the disciples breathe in fresh piquancy of the open air. We have moved through the streets. The more immediate smells of daily life—rubbish, animal waste, even the odor of human excrement—alert us to the reality of daily life in a town. These more basic encounters are relieved when we come to Gethsemane. The smell we experience now is clearer. There is a mixture of the dry and the moist. There are hints of wood, grass, herbs and budding flowers as we join Jesus as he kneels in the garden.

For some of the apostles their consciousness remains with the feast. There is a tinge of the smell of the banquet on their clothes.

Traces of food and wine may be in the beard. But overall it is the freshness of being outdoors. There is the smell of spring, of a verdancy as yet not burned by the sun. Yet even those sensations are fleeting. Tiredness overcomes the apostles and their sense of smell evaporates in sleep.

In anxiety Jesus breathes hard. The knowledge of his betrayal dominates all Jesus' senses. Our Lord asks the Father to undo what he knows is being played out. The smell of turf and blossom are lost. Jesus is oblivious to their pleasurable fragrance. Placing some distance between them and himself, Jesus prays. Jesus prays from his own expectation, his knowledge of what is to follow.

> *Abba, Father, for you all things are possible; remove this cup from me; yet not what I want, but what you want.* (Mark 14:36)

The anxiety, the pain and, though we often ignore it, the fear of what was to follow detracts from the rich fragrances around Jesus. The emotions welling inside Jesus create a physical barrier. They get in the way. Maybe they even conspire to obliterate what nature is proclaiming to Jesus. One's own situation can wipe out the external world. Perhaps the smell of fear blocked the nostrils of Jesus.

The Scent of Hostility and Betrayal

The inhibition of Jesus' own senses is curtailed by the approach of the crowd. Signs of their imminent arrival could be discerned in the air. There is a smell of oil and fire as those who come to arrest Jesus carry torches to hold off the descending gloom. The scent of the flames would be intensified if the breeze was blowing behind the crowd as it made its way into the garden. Within the crowd is a mixture of odors. There is the smell of the people themselves and what they carry. There is a mixture of aromas of cloth and leather. For some, moving in such a diverse group is an affront. The unwashed can offend those of more delicate sensibilities. We know the crowd was made up of those from humble and exalted stations. High priests and scribes were among their number. The relative luxury of their lives gives a different perfume to that of the crowd. There is an acrid smell of sweat in the air as the excited, jostling people press on. Individuals are straining in the effort to keep up with the events, not to miss any development. Through this comes the polished smell of the military. Well-preserved tanned leather, the whiff of oil on metal, as the soldiers lead and restrain the crowd at the same time. Jesus could have discerned one or many of these individual smells. Yet the main alarm was in the corporate odor that a large group was coming.

From the amassed smells comes one with singular strength. It is a peculiarly personal smell. It becomes the intimate aroma of betrayal. It is the smell of Judas as he moves his face toward Jesus. There is a pause before he kisses Jesus. It is amid this closeness that each man can communicate with the other in a way none of the crowd can. They can smell the breath of the one standing opposite. After the kiss, it is this aroma which our Lord savors before he is taken away. That close contact of breath to breath. Then Jesus is seized, held, pinioned and he gasps, taking in the aggressive scent of others as he is led away to torture, judgment and death.

The Atmosphere of the Trials

Jesus is usually depicted as being in the forefront of the processions to the trials. Jesus has passed through the crush of sweaty bodies to gain relatively clear air. This allows Jesus a certain freedom, which continues in his hearings before the Sanhedrin and Pilate. Jesus stands in isolation some way from his accusers. But there are subtle changes to the atmosphere. There is a preponderance of the well-off in the first trial. Jesus faces the high priests. As Jesus stands before the high priest, Caiaphas, the smell of the crowd is not immediately apparent to him. It serves more as a sensual backdrop.

There are changes when Jesus is taken from there to the court of Pontius Pilate. Again we rely on depictions of the scent in art to suggest other sensual experiences. Here is the imposing smell of foreignness. Alien powers tend to assert their distinctiveness from local cultures in many ways. Food is cooked to remind colonial workers of home. This wafts into the open areas around the court. But in the more formal areas, these are kept at bay. We assume scrubbed surfaces. There is a spit-and-polish aura round the chief representative of the imperial power in Jerusalem. In this Jesus is very much alone.

When Pilate orders Jesus' scourging, there is a series of sudden shocks. The sweat and leather of the soldier is forced on Jesus as

Jesus is grabbed, bound and beaten. Jesus is aware, in an unavoidable closeness, of the personal smells of these fighting men. Can Jesus detect an enjoyment in an enthusiastic compliance with their orders to beat him? Jesus smells them in front of him. As the scourge slashes Jesus' back, his awareness of others is distracted. Jesus' nostrils clog with mucus as his body too tries to block out the pain being inflicted on him. Jesus collapses. His senses clear for a moment. Jesus is brought around with his face in the dirt. A foot comes near, and its odor a mixture of leather and dirty feet diminishes as Jesus is hauled up again to receive more brutal treatment. Something is held under Jesus' nose. Jesus makes a futile attempt to identify it. It is whisked away and the crown of thorns is thrust on Jesus' head. The smell of cloth hits Jesus' nostrils. He realizes that whatever he is wearing, it is not his own. It has been wrapped round him as part of the mocked acclamation of him as King of the Jews.

Smelling the Approach of Death

After this Jesus is mostly the victim of others' direction. The sights, sounds and smells come to Jesus as he treads the gruesome road to Golgotha. First Jesus is led onto the open street. Released from the confines of the barracks, Jesus is now restricted by his own body. The weight of the cross cramps Jesus' muscles first and in time impairs all his senses. How many of the smells of the street, the enticing and revolting, would Jesus have noticed as he struggled with the weight of the cross? Carrying the cross is hefty work. Yet there are times when the surroundings insist we take note of them. Even people driving in a car with sealed windows will note the acrid indications of manure-spreading in rural areas. The smells are unavoidable. There must be times, despite the cruelty of what he is undergoing, when Jesus is keenly aware of the street.

The biggest barrier is a personal one. There is a sourness when one's own exertion exudes a pungency which affects the self and others differently. People playing high-energy sports every now and then find themselves embarrassed because of the almost overpowering nature of their own body odor. People working on building sites sometimes express the same dismay. Jesus' effort would have had a physical expression, an expression in the smell of sweat. This would, of course, be most acute to those near the Lord. The guards and others in the procession would have known more of the agony of Jesus because they could smell what was going on. For those further back, those looking on from a distance, the experience was a different one.

The sharing of smell incorporates a physical proximity. We are able to share in some of those intimate contacts through the Stations of the Cross. These contacts have a two-way quality. We can engage in an exchange of personal scent. This is particularly so in one of the stations which has its base in scripture.

As they led him away, they seized a man, Simon of Cyrene, who was coming from the country, and they laid the cross on him, and made him carry it behind Jesus. (Luke 23:26)

For a part of the journey, and we do not know how long or short a part it is, Simon has to do battle with his own scent. We can only assume he was chosen because he looked fit and strong. He trails behind a person who has been beaten and abused. It is significant that Simon is mentioned in the gospel narratives very soon after the end of the trial. The rigor of what Jesus has undergone has sapped Jesus' energy. Yet Simon does not concentrate his attention on Jesus. He is too distracted by the weight of the cross. It is safe to assume that Simon's awareness would be on something more immediate than the person in front of him.

It is a powerful irony that a passerby is drawn in to experience the activity of the main player. It is worth remembering that our shared senses allow us to have a part in what is happening. We cannot substitute ourselves for another. But our senses, especially our imaginative use of them, give us access to part of what can occur. The nostrils of Simon of Cyrene, however, by his carrying of the cross, have a unique impression of the pain of Jesus. An outsider is brought in to share an intimate aspect of the Passion.

Jesus, on the other hand, is temporarily freed from this toil. Jesus' senses are liberated. Jesus is able to smell the wider world. The crush of the crowd is still distant but discernible. Ironically this reprieve alerts Jesus to the constraints he is subject to. Jesus becomes more acutely aware of the military. Our Lord gets a whiff of the polished metal. It is the odor of the instrument of the clean brutality of the militarist mind. Tools, dress, equipment and person are kept in the cleanest state of readiness to allow them to be dirtied in the most gruesome fashion. The freshness of aroma, a piquancy of cleanliness is a signal of preparedness to wallow in filth in a way few other occupations will allow.

At this point Jesus also comes into contact with those beyond the border of control that is represented and made real by the soldiers. There are three poignant encounters with women in the Stations of the Cross. In many ways they are the touchstones of care and concern in such a meditation. In all other activities men are in the forefront. It is a man who betrays Jesus. Men gather to give evidence against Jesus and other men sit in judgment upon Jesus. Apart from Pontius Pilate, who desperately attempts to find a method through which Jesus can be spared, men jostle for Jesus' condemnation. This is not to suggest all men did so. Peter, for instance, regretted his act of denial. Others in the crowds which followed the event of the Passion must have been revolted. They must have opposed what was happening. It is salutary to recall that crowds, however homogeneous their behavior, are constituted of individuals. A crowd reaction is, therefore, a conglomerate reaction. But within this crowd Simon of Cyrene, albeit compelled to take part, is the only man who is specifically drawn as sympathetic to Jesus' plight.

How different are the reactions of women! And there is a fragrance to these encounters. It is the fragrance of compassion, pity and empathy. Jesus meets women in the fourth, sixth and eighth stations. The first two, which we will consider, are apocryphal. The final incident, the meeting of the women of Jerusalem, is recorded in scripture.

When Jesus meets his mother, she receives the full impact of the prediction made by Simeon in the temple. His words recorded in the Gospel of Luke come true. Having acknowledged Jesus as the fulfillment of the expectation of Israel, the righteous and devout man, who was looking for the consolation of Israel, gave the mother of the babe a warning.

> *This child is destined for the falling and the rising of many in Israel, and to be a sign that will be opposed so that the inner thoughts of many will be revealed—and a sword will pierce your own soul too.* (Luke 2:34-35)

Mary sees her child and smells doom. It is easy to imagine Mary sensing all that has gone on. The indignities meted out upon Jesus' flesh are apparent to her. She is also aware that worse is to come. There is a numbness in all of Jesus' senses as Jesus looks into the eyes of Mary. This scene is often rendered with some distance between the parent and child. They stand back from each other. This is in contrast to the closeness of depicted scenes of the Lord's birth or childhood. Most famous must be the Madonna and Child, the pictures of Mary holding the infant Christ. The next time they are portrayed in such proximity is after the death of Jesus. This intimacy is classically captured in the Pietà image—the grieving mother cradles the corpse of her adult son. The Pietà is rendered evocatively and most famously by Michelangelo.

The next encounter with a woman is a gesture of kindness. In Veronica's action of wiping Jesus' face, Jesus is allowed to rid himself of some of the accretion of suffering. Though Jesus may hurt and feel pain in many ways, suddenly his sense of smell is cleared. Perhaps, even only for a moment, Jesus is freed to take in the surrounding plethora of events. This is achieved in a simple gesture of concern, the drying of the Lord's face. Many paintings of this display the moment as one of shared pain. Veronica stands holding the cloth which has just passed over the contours of the face of our Lord. It now carries a complete imprint of Jesus' visage. It captures this in the blood, tears, sweat and dirt of Jesus' walk to Golgotha. There is an exchange in this. Veronica tends to the suffering man despite Jesus' pungent odor. Jesus exudes the smells of dirt, abuse, sweat and filth. Jesus carries the smells which he himself has expressed. They have developed as a result of what has happened to him. Many of these are on Jesus' face and these are all collected on the relatively odor-free cloth. It is this collection of smell, in the fluids of the human body, which artists are trying to capture. In this way the imprinted face of the suffering Savior is not literal but metaphorical. Our Lord's very being is caught in his experience which Veronica has absorbed into the fabric. What remains on the towel is the smell of the man on his way to death.

From this point the senses of the onlookers gain precedence. Most of those watching have been held back from Jesus. Unlike the women or Simon of Cyrene, they have not encountered the odors of this deathly walk. Held back for purposes of security, people in the crowd are more aware of the smells around them. Just as being close to the action is rewarded with a good view, distance deadens the olfactory experience. Not being able to detect the degradation to which Jesus has been subjected, they can enjoy the spectacle. Because of this, the smell of the crowd, the street, the animals takes on a vibrancy: there is an almost tangible smell of excitement. For them the end of this journey is the vindication in seeing a criminal, a blasphemer, go to death.

No such distraction is available to those who are nearby. As Jesus pushes on to the ultimate destinations, Golgotha and death, they can sense the fullness of human suffering in a way those distant cannot. In many ways, the necessary description of the death of our Lord as torturous is making it safe. But contemplation of the sheer physical stress involved in Jesus' ordeal forces us to confront what we might otherwise think of as unsavory aspects. The pain, exertion and anxiety make real the physical. Blood, mucus, urine and feces are real expressions of the body when it is suffering so intensely. For those unused to such ordeals, such odors would be and are disturbing, a sensual signal of how vicious a death this person is undergoing. For those for whom execution was their occupation, a psychological distancing would have been built-in. We know this from contemporary society. It is simply seen among people on whose work we rely. People involved in emergency services, those employed in sewage works, even those in caring professions, develop a way to deal with events and personal situations which would otherwise overpower casual onlookers. This is not to suggest they are callous or impervious to what they encounter, just that they recognize what is occurring for what it is, and thereby set about whatever task is required of them.

It is this commixture of scents, the real, final suffering smells of humanity, which emanates from the cross. Never is it more apparent that Christianity depends on the humanity of the Godhead. In many depictions of the nativity of Christ all the pain, stress, agony and physical reality of birth is done away with. The Virgin Mary kneels in veneration of her son. This may be an unconscious extension of the peculiar thinking which resulted in such pronouncements as that the Virgin Mary did not suffer from the pains of childbirth. This places her apart from the condemned Eve and her daughters. So does the bizarre medieval claim that Mary's hymen remained intact after the birth of the Savior child. The power of the Incarnation is in the reality of humanity. That involves the reality of birth and, in considering the Passion, the reality of death.

Yet for the person at the center of this amazing story of birth, life, death and salvation, the stench of death is remote. Jesus' sense of smell is blocked off. The body's methods of dealing with all this torment are to void itself and to provide buffers. So Jesus, whose sense of smell embraces so much, of others, of himself, is ultimately disconnected from that vital element of life—air. And it is that element, the breath of life, through Jesus' mouth and Jesus' nose, which proclaims the arrival of the transforming act, the act through which salvation is made known.

EXERCISES

1. Sit comfortably in your chair. Close your eyes and breathe. Now proceed with a basic Yoga exercise. Those suffering from a cold may want to pass on this one! Place your hand to your face with a thumb and forefinger to each nostril. Block the passage of air into one nostril and breathe in through the other. Exhale. Then ease the pressure on the blocked nostril, and restrict your breathing on the other side. Breathe in and out. Repeat this alternating procedure for ten breaths through each nostril.

2. Staying where you are, focus your sense of smell. Try to become aware of what odors are:

- about your person—try to identify them, where the may have their source;
- on your chair;
- in the room;
- if a window is open, the fragrances coming into the room from outside.

Think where these scents become part of each other. Imagine a border between them.

3. If in a group, pass the following objects about. If alone, smell each

in turn. Remember, do not rush, and try not to discuss your reactions until all members of the group have had the opportunity to smell them:

- a rose;
- a bar of scented soap;
- a glass of water;
- an orange;
- a glass of wine;
- finally, your fingers which have handled all these things.

4. Light some incense in the room. If in a group, discuss reactions to the aroma as it increases. Say what memories it evokes, if any. After this, sit silently or pray.

QUESTIONS FOR REFLECTION AND DISCUSSION

1. God's gift of smell enriches our lives more than we realize. For instance, what memories are evoked when you sniff the scent of freshly baked bread? Newly mown grass?

2. What are some odors that stir our fears, our negative emotions? The smell of something burning? An aroma of decay? The scent of hospitals or sickrooms?

3. The author points out that distance deadens or reduces our sense of smell. Do we distance ourselves from the horrors of Jesus' trial and crucifixion? How do we place psychological distance between

ourselves and others so that we cannot "smell" their fear and pain?

4. Genesis 2:7 tells us that "the LORD God . . . breathed into his nostrils the breath of life; and the man became a living being." How can we become more aware that our breath is part of the very Breath of God? How does that connection affect our relationships with others and with God?

5. Sing aloud or silently the hymn: "Breathe on me, Breath of God, fill me with life anew, that I may love what Thou dost love, and do what Thou wouldst do." As you breathe in this profound petition, allow God to speak a personal word to your heart.

*Eternal God, we thank you for the myriad signs
of your creation which we detect in our sense of smell.
May we relish those gifts which communicate their beauty
in a way that enhances them. We give thanks for our
enjoyment of flowers and gardens, for the delight we sense
in cooking. We also ask that we do not turn from the more
unpleasant aspects of life communicated through this sense.
May we use this gift to inform ourselves of what is
about us and, where we can, to act to correct any decay.
We ask this through Jesus Christ our Lord. Amen.*

Who Touched Me?

Have you ever thought how touching the Passion of Jesus is? I do not mean in the sense of moving your emotions, although the Passion can be very touching that way. But have you considered how tactile the stories of Christ's last hours are?

In a culture where the tactile is often said to be discouraged, we need to look more closely at what we say when we extend ourselves through touch. We should pause to consider how we communicate with our sense of touch. There is a clichéd allegation that, in some sections of our society anyway, touch is at risk of being divorced from everyday emotion. That is to say we reserve it for extremes such as the closeness of lovemaking or for the violence of assault. But does that claim have any evidence to support it?

All cultures use touch to express ideas and emotions. There are formal greetings and acknowledgments which can carry an inner meaning. The quality of a person's handshake can communicate to you more than the mere ritual of the greeting on its own. If it is solid and hearty, it may be telling you that the other person is very glad to see you. Or you may discern something else, a presentiment, a reluctance to discuss anything of depth with you. This may be passed on through a wet-fish handshake, a dropping limp hand that fails to connect fully with yours. Or the opposite of the apparent message may be behind the gesture. A solid hug can be used as a defense from intimacy. It may be a signal to say "Please do not inquire within."

And there are degrees of expression really known only to participants. Kissing can inform both those so engaged and others watching of the nature of the relationship between the kissers. A couple in the throes of newly discovered love and passion do not kiss in the same way as a young man might kiss his grandmother.

This range of tactile expression can even extend to inanimate objects. Watch a person pat a seat next to him when he wants you to move close to him so he can share some secret with you. We can see more than stoic acceptance in the way an actor can hold aloft a statue like an Oscar. Or how an Olympic athlete can clutch the gold medal which has just been hung round her neck. The gesture, the way the actor or the athlete touches the object, informs us of the anxiety, the work, the effort, even the sheer good luck it has taken to bring him or her to the moment of glory.

We use our sense of touch both as an outward and an inward communicator. We give out messages and we receive them with our bodies. We know when a loved one is angry, upset, distraught, by the stiffness in his or her frame. This information is felt by our hands and communicates on a deep level. We can feel the jubilation, nervousness or doubt in someone else's hands, back or limbs. Touch is used routinely to gather and give out all sorts of information.

Sometimes we feel linked, we feel our sense of touch react, when we merely observe others. Violence in a film can make an audience gasp. It gasps because those watching have an intuitive physical response to what they see. They can feel an empathy with a person on the screen. So too can those watching an event be involved indirectly through their sense of touch. If an athlete falls while going full speed in a race, we can feel, albeit through our assumed or intuitive relationship, some of the jolt which brings him to the ground when he trips. When we see an errant kick on the soccer field we are able to share the "Ouch!" of the player whose shins have been assaulted. We unconsciously use our imagination when we see other people hesitating in their touch, with things or with people. A gesture may be withheld because the person extending the arm to someone in distress is unsure, so the arm is drawn back. We can see that the person on the edge of making the gesture is afraid of the consequences, of how to deal with where a reassuring touch may lead.

We can also feel pain, react to its possibility, even if we do not directly witness the person-to-person contact involved. It is possible to feel the pain, share the agony of an accident, merely through someone relating the story of its occurrence. Faces squint, breath is expelled, sometimes we even rub the part affected in an incident involving not us, but the person on whom the anecdote centers.

It is no surprise, then, that touch is one part which makes up the fullness of the Passion. Knowing that all the participants in the final hours of Jesus shared our senses, however differently we may choose or have to use them nowadays, reminds us that touch is part of the total sensual experience of the Passion. The accounts of the

Last Supper contain many incidents of touch: from the closest, almost intimate contact, to the other extreme, a distance which speaks of a presentiment of physical violence; and the complete withdrawal of touch which makes us focus on the aloneness of Jesus at the end of the path he walked to Golgotha.

Again, we must remind ourselves of the dividing lines involved. On the one hand, it is the touch of Jesus we must concentrate on. We will consider what Jesus felt, what was done to Jesus' flesh and body. And likewise there will be tactile sentient experience of others. We will attempt to experience what they felt directly or by virtue of their imaginations as they watched what occurred to Jesus. How touch affected them as they watched a person move from trial and condemnation to execution.

The Washing of Feet

The first exchange of touch occurs at the Last Supper. What is presumed routine is turned on its head by Jesus. Preparation to eat, even with the advantages of cutlery, usually involves the washing of hands. This seemingly commonsensical habit has echoes in cultic and ritual behavior. Many faiths insist on ritual washing before entering sacred spaces. Many priests wash their hands before proceeding into the eucharistic prayer at Holy Communion, using a version of a prayer from the Psalms:

I wash my hands in innocence, and go around your altar, O LORD. (Psalm 26:6)

Jewish food laws make much of ritual cleansing—not just the washing of people, but of the utensils used for the preparation and serving of food. They affect what is to be eaten, how it will be killed, cooked and served, as well as those who will eat it. There are rules as to which food is clean or otherwise. The Law articulates the codes which say whether people are clean or unclean. It informs as to what events can make someone unclean and what must be done in order to make oneself fit again for food and worship. The Jewish leaders were often at odds with Jesus and the disciples over these rules. One of the reasons for suspicion of the disciples was that they did not wash themselves according to the Law. Jesus' startling response to one challenge at this lack of observance was to look to the inner person for the assessment of cleanliness.

There is nothing outside a person that by going in can defile, but the things that come out are what defile. (Mark 7:15)

Despite these controversies well before the Passion events, washing is central to preparation for the Last Supper. But when washing occurs it is very unusual. We feel the normal pecking order upended. The Master, the Lord, is washing the feet of the followers. The disciples pull back in shock as water poured from a jug splashes on their feet. They feel its coolness catching on the dust of the street. They react to the startling sensation of Jesus washing off the dirt, the rinsing clean before the comparatively harsh rub of the towel. They feel Jesus' hands speak to them through their feet. They become aware of parts of their bodies they may have ignored. The followers feel hands on their flesh, their toenails. A gentle hand touches a sore, a callous, a scar.

In many churches this incident is ritualistically represented every Maundy Thursday. The minister of the Eucharist lays aside the finery and kneels before other celebrant members of the church, washing their feet. It is a ceremony which is both moving and revolting. Those who have agreed or been selected to take part often wonder if their feet will be good enough. Some even anticipate the event by giving their toes a good scrub before the occasion. It is as though, while taking a role, they would like to distance themselves (especially when the priest goes so far as to kiss the feet), from this rather unsavory piece of theater. These reactions capture the response of the disciples. Peter, so outraged by this spectacle of his teacher on his knees before him, points out that Jesus is the leader. Jesus, as he does do often in the Gospels, then rebukes Peter for missing the point:

Jesus answered, "Unless I wash you, you have no share with me." Simon Peter said to him, "Lord, not my feet only but also my hands and my head!" Jesus said to him, "One who has bathed does not need to wash, except for the feet, but is entirely clean." (John 13:8-10)

Why did Jesus concentrate on feet? Anyone who is easily tickled will tell you of the extreme sensitivity of the feet, of how the lightest stroke on them can reverberate through the body. This is also borne out by therapy such as reflexology. The techniques of reflexology concentrate on pressure points on the foot. It is believed that concentrated pressure on a particular area of the sole of the foot can have a beneficial effect elsewhere in the body. Such therapy can be a surprise.

So much of our thinking ignores the feet. It can take unusual circumstances for them to come to our attention. They get us from one place to another. Anyone who has undergone a long, hard walk in the country on a hot day will recognize the luxuriant freshness to be enjoyed after washing the feet. Your feet seem to be throbbing in the joy of cleanliness. By concentrating on them, by feeling the feet washed and dried, the disciples saw their mobility, a part of themselves not usually included in the ritual washing, as a new focus.

The Hands of Jesus

The feet of the disciples having been attended to, the meal continues with hands breaking bread and passing around this special meal. Parts of the disciples' bodies, their feet, are now hidden beneath the table. They are clean, but the strange reversal of authority is now shown by the hands of Jesus as Jesus moves on to clean what cannot be seen.

In many classic pictures of the Last Supper, always somewhat unreliable because of their stagelike layout with everyone sitting on one side of the table, we can see many of the contact points between the apostles. These contacts can have a secondary use. They can connect Jesus and us. Let us start on the outer fringes of the picture. Usually there are some apostles leaning in, hunched over, gripping the table, almost clawing the surfaces as they press together. They literally rub up against each other. Cloth touches cloth. Cloth makes contact with skin. Body is pressed against body. What is it that gives rise to such urgency? They press and push to get closer to Jesus. They are vying for an unrestricted view. Or they want to hear what Jesus is saying more clearly. Whatever the reason, they express themselves physically to achieve their goals. They communicate these needs through their bodies.

The crush of person upon person indicates an urgency, almost a desperation, to be involved. You can imagine the consequences: upsetting the tableware, perhaps the spilling of someone's drink, the subsequent feel of dampness on fingers, a splash between bare toes, crumbs caught under the palm, the accidental kicking of feet under the table, the push back to repel the overenthusiasm of one of their number.

And in the center there is usually one of two scenes. Both are intimate and both are essential to our relationship to our Lord. And yet their essential quality, though similar, expresses a different understanding in each case. The Last Supper is a connection between Christ and Christ's followers then, and is a link for today. It connects Christ to us. The sacrament of Holy Communion recaptures, enacts, the Last Supper for us each and every time we participate in it. Yet it captures more than a memorial meal. It captures the whole Christian story. Vital to it is this, the taking, blessing and breaking of bread. To that end, in the first of these two images, we often see Christ holding the bread.

Having washed the disciples' feet, Jesus' hands are now the center of the action. The simple touch of a hand on a baked loaf, the deceptively easy event, carries a plethora of messages. For the apostles they were being communicated to by Jesus taking the bread in his hands. We have a fuller knowledge than the apostles at the Last Supper. We know the entire saving Passion of Jesus. We celebrate it every time at the Eucharist. We do this knowing that Jesus has spoken to us personally and in a tangible way. We have been touched.

How often do you *feel* your food? Our culture tends to discourage this, especially for more formal meals. Perhaps it does so for good reason. Cutlery arguably allows for an enhanced degree of hygiene. But it can and does provide a barrier between that which we have done and that which we are doing. It separates the residue of dirt and experience on our hands from the moving of our food to our mouths.

Anyone who has traveled in a culture where food is routinely eaten "hand to mouth"—the noble sandwich becomes a poor second in such consideration—may experience the jolt of joy, surprise or revulsion when hands feel, even swim in, the food. The breaking of bread, the tearing of a loaf, which Jesus does with his own hands, captures a multitude of symbols. The telling of this story, for us who have knowledge of the aftermath, can trigger other stories—

that Jesus' followers will know Jesus in the breaking of bread. We have our Lord tearing that which will symbolize, will be, the reminder, the presence of Jesus among his disciples, among us. And that is tender. It is touching.

The apostles then feel the bread passed into their own hands, as we feel the sacrament when it is placed in ours. It has texture. It has weight. Having sensed the tearing of their leader, they feel the rough edge, the crumbling boundary and take it and place to their mouths. There are sensations on the lips, scratchy yet smooth, in the mouth, on the teeth, in the throat. These are all vital to eating and all have their own unmistakable physical sensations. There is the solidity of the cup as it passes from hand to hand, perhaps with a hint of wetness, evidence of a slurp from the person before. And there is the cool, moist interchange as the wine meets their lips.

The Breast of Jesus

The second traditional central image of a painting of the Last Supper is also touching. The tactile aspect of the scene is a more particular closeness because it expresses a private intimacy. It is the touch between persons rather than communication through things. John, the disciple Jesus loved, lies, depending on the artist, in an attitude of love, closeness, desolation, exhaustion, even drunkenness, on the chest of our Lord. In this intimate gathering, this select coming together to share a meal of celebration and pain, there is a personal closeness available. We become like John, nestled on the breast of our teacher. Like John, we feel our hand brush against the fabric of Jesus' tunic, the bristling of his beard. Our head lifts with the rise and fall of the Master's breath. We become aware of Jesus' changing gestures. We sense, in a way none of the others at the table can, that Jesus is becoming tense. We know Jesus is aware of something monumental, something which is altering Jesus' physical being. We lift our head from Jesus' chest, we feel the panting breath on our face in response to the awful suggestion that among us is a traitor. From that vantage point we ask the searching, searing question:

Surely, not I? (Mark 14:19)

Muscular tension spreads, as though it is an infection. There is a stiffening of sinews at the same time, in advance of the realization that one among our number is going to allow our leader to be given over. To what? There is a tightening in the body as each thinks: Is my closeness, my touch, to be the denial, the act of betrayal? That question can be answered in a tactile fashion. Indeed it is. The moment following this reply is caught in several artistic depictions of the scene. Along with all the other apostles, pressing in, crouching in at the extremities, stands one in a special relationship. Paintings often assist us by showing him standing to one side, apart, ready to leave. He has heard the response to John's question and is to fulfill the role. But the touching revelation of his function in the crucifixion story happens moments before this commonly portrayed point of departure. Along with all the others, Judas Iscariot leans in, brushes his hands against our Lord, taking a moist piece of bread with his fingers, only to find his muscles stiffen as the sentence is pronounced:

The one who has dipped his hand into the bowl with me will betray me. (Matthew 26:23)

This is a solemn reminder. Our fellowship with Jesus, our ongoing contact, must be guarded, cherished and cared for. We could easily allow contact to remain casual. We could let it be a mere brushing up against Jesus. But it is our task to continue our work in and through this contact. Even the elect are at risk. Even during something as solemn and wonderful as the common and extraordinary memorial meal.

The Kiss of Judas

Judas's next action in the Passion narratives is even more tactile. Arriving with the crowd he touches his Master with an ironic gesture. He uses a greeting, an act of affection and love to betray the Lord. The brush of lips upon cheek is the signal for the pains and agony of Jesus to begin. The kiss itself is a bridge from one person to another, of body to body. Yet it heralds a series of harsh physical actions upon the flesh of our Lord. But before the physical actions and activities take place on and within the body of Jesus, Jesus asks the disciple:

Judas, is it with a kiss that you are betraying the Son of Man? (Luke 22:48)

We know he is. And so much of the answer to that question was, could only be, expressed in physical terms. Jesus' life ended brutally. And what took place just after the betrayal was brutal. Jesus was grabbed by those eager to complete a task which had been set in motion hours, days, months before. And among the people who had come along to witness the arrest were many keen to see how Jesus' supporters would react. Violence erupted quickly. Swords were pulled from scabbards. Blows were rained on people on both sides of the camp. Pain was felt, blood was drawn. This mayhem was brought to a halt by the person at the center of the controversy. Jesus raised his hand, urging his followers to put their swords away. This command with its inherent rebuke had a bodily impact. The shame involved, the risk being run, halted in a stiffness, a knowledge that the actions carried out did not express, could only fail to express, the high regard for the person now taken prisoner.

Jesus Manhandled

So much of what follows can only be felt. Jesus is grabbed. Jesus' arms pinch as they feel the burn of a firm restraint. Jesus' skin smarts because of that overzealous grip of soldiers who want to fulfill their duty. Perhaps these military men even relish the opportunity to display power afforded by their duties. Yet theirs is really an intermediary role. They confine the prisoner, restrain the crowds, keep out unwanted interference, but do so at the behest of someone else. Their hands are the physical extensions of the minds and decisions of other people: people who rely on the translation of policy into hand-to-body contact. The soldiers' actions are most easily achieved by a firm resolve, expressed to the world in hands, arms and physical strength.

In the court of Pontius Pilate, Jesus experiences relative freedom. Some pictures of this scene show Jesus bound, Jesus' hands caught in the grip of ropes which, however gently applied, cause great discomfort and, in time, agony. Or was Jesus released? Were the firm bands eased from the Master's muscles? Were the mere confines of the building and the court restraint enough? But even this relative freedom can be oppressive. Jesus is usually pictured alone. Our Lord is isolated from the crush of the excited mob. A protective cordon has been placed around Jesus by the military. The jostling and shoving by which Jesus has been directed and redirected has halted. Jesus is now on his own.

In this solitary standing Jesus' body would be giving Jesus more tactile information. When people are worried they speak of the world weighing on their shoulders. It is as though their inner concerns, often about matters external to them, things over which they have no control, become a physical burden. They can feel their anxiety. It speaks through stiffened muscles. The body complains that it is not at ease. Despite Jesus' knowledge of what was to befall and why, did Jesus bring this tension of his prayers in Gethsemane with him?

The isolation is interrupted by a brutal interlude. Jesus is grabbed, manhandled, Jesus' arms set to a post. The Master's muscles tense as he hears the swish of the lash and then the report in and through his flesh that the whip has hit home. It is generally thought this kind of flagellation was as gruesome as it could be. Prisoners treated in this way are regularly reported to have died as a result of it. The lash was multitongued, probably with cutting edges of bone and metal embedded to inflict the most ghastly and efficient cuts. But sensation would not have been in Christ's back alone. There is the tug on the wrist as Jesus drops under the lash, his knees crashing into the earth. Perhaps soldiers grapple with Jesus to make him stand to receive the punishment. And Jesus would feel the throb of the blood coursing in his face and head. This torture was ordered in a mis-judged effort by Pontius Pilate to arouse pity. It was done as part of a judicial process. Jesus feels the smart of spit, blows and the lash as part of a system of justice. It is clear, in the various gospel accounts, that this all happens while the judicial process—or attempts to thwart or affect the judicial process—is being carried out.

We rely on others to make our laws for us. We empower people to enact regulations and legislation on our behalf. We hope these will be enforced and administered by the police and the courts. We ask people to hold these offices for us on trust. We want them to act on our behalf. And so much of our justice depends on the way others exercise this trust—for good or ill. Our justice depends on how they perform for us.

It is this abuse which is meted out to Jesus. Pontius Pilate's plan was to thwart the mob's excitement. He was seeking their pity. He was hoping to elicit a common feeling with a suffering individual. But still the popular outcry continued, beseeching him to have Jesus crucified. Realizing his tactics had failed, Pilate relents. Jesus is once again manhandled to walk the painful road to Golgotha.

The Feel of the Cross

We now know this is redeeming suffering. We feel the Passion through the relief and wonder of the resurrection. We know that, through this human pain, God was acting to reconcile this world to the eternal. But any consideration of these final hours of Jesus can best be felt as shared suffering. This is human pain. A pain we all share. A pain we all have a part in. This is where we join our Savior in the Christian story. And the reverse is true. God suffers with humanity because God suffered as a human. No more real is the link between eternal and the temporal than in pain. The heavy weight of pain is borne out, some would say dragged out, in the Stations of the Cross, which can be seen on the walls of many churches.

Of the traditional fourteen stations, we will consider three incidents. The first is from the second station, the taking of the cross. This is worth looking at because it incorporates many of the others. For without Jesus first taking the cross, without bearing it on his shoulders, feeling its weight on and through his back, his entire body, no other station matters.

When Jesus took the cross he had already suffered a series of enervating indignities. Jesus had been hit, partly through play in mockery, partly through viciousness in the torture of the scourging. Jesus had been spat upon. One person's body fluid was used to assault another. Jesus had been jostled by the crowd. Jesus had been protected from it by the bodies and weapons of men from whose number his tormentors would later come. When Jesus came to take the cross he was exhausted. The Master was lucky to have survived what had occurred, only to live through the worse that was to follow.

The acceptance of a load is deceptive. Even something as relatively mundane as picking up a bag of groceries at the supermarket can be surprising. At first the weight is not a challenge. Indeed, it may appear very light. But as the walk continues, as we struggle not with the bag itself but the dead weight of its contents, we start to flag. The load seems to become heavier than it was.

For Jesus the load is thrust on shoulders which are smarting already from the injuries sustained. Jesus can feel the rough wood locate the wounds, rubbing areas which had until then escaped the hurt. And Jesus also feels, through the contact of wood on flesh, the weight. Our Lord starts out with reduced strength and it is with these diminished reserves he must battle on. In the Stations of the Cross we know that the battle is a difficult one: that is signified by the three falls. As the Lord attempts to keep going, harassed, pressed in on, receiving the occasional jab of encouragement or abuse, his body reminds him that it is not just his shoulders which bear the load. Under the crippling weight, Jesus' feet scuff the road, thud heavily as Jesus fights to stay upright. Jesus absorbs the shocks in his knees, locking them to stymie collapse. Jesus' back complains that it is bent. It cannot straighten itself to find release into physical freedom. Jesus feels himself lurch back and forth. This battle continues, and Jesus' muscles send his brain the message that the struggle has been in vain. Jesus' legs give out beneath him, his knees crack on the ground as Jesus crumples into the earth.

Even the temporary reprieve from this exhausted state is illusory. Jesus is hauled up, begrudgingly assisted to take the load again and the madness starts once more. Yet mitigation of a sort does come. In the second incident, the fifth station, Simon of Cyrene is compelled to carry the cross for Jesus. This physical hiatus stops short of relief to the battered and bruised body of the condemned man. But Simon's action is significant because it allows the pain of Jesus to be shared. For however long Simon is involved, he provides an insight to Jesus' suffering because he carries the weight of the cross. Jesus, now freed from the external load, still has his own pain from the jolts, the stiffness and soreness to carry. Part of Jesus' burden has been spread but ultimately, as the Stations of the Cross so graphically show, the ordeal remains Jesus' and Jesus' alone.

In all this we feel the parody of the Last Supper images of people eager to get a better view, pushing others out of the way to achieve their objective. There is confusion here as the enthusiastic followers rub up against those trying to escape, those who want to place some distance between the barbarity of justice and the personal pain it entails, and others who see but cannot believe.

The third incident is the most graphically and terrifyingly physical. Jesus is nailed to the cross. Much of the Christian heritage depends on three nails. These three nails are essential to the eleventh station. Their place in the Christian heritage is secure because the nails are the central reminder of it all. The nails themselves, simple and useful in their many applications, are turned to the most vivid, the most cruel, the most potent expression of pain. A highly telling example of this is the simple combination which makes up the Cross of Nails in Coventry Cathedral. The nails become the cross. The symbol of the cross, however it is created, tells us of more than death. It is also the symbol of the redemption of humanity. Christ's death, prolonged, agonizing and painful, has a positive purpose. It is a declaration of freedom.

Jesus feels a new kind of contact with the cross as his arms are stretched. Any accustomed feeling with the wood is banished as Jesus' arms are yanked apart. The backs of Jesus' wrists are slapped onto the crossbar. Jesus' muscles are in spasm as they fight against involuntary contraction. On the journey up the hill, in the effort required to hold the cross, Jesus' sinews have taken the mold. Relieved of that burden, the body seeks a shape in which relief is felt. These efforts are checked as Jesus feels firm, rough hands encircle his wrists and bash them back to the wood. Jesus feels his fingers torn open as they try to make a protective fist. Any struggle brings a coarse, restraining weight. Jesus is being crushed between flesh and wood.

On one wrist a third hand moves into place as his executioner comes into contact with the battered body of a man. The executioner has a job to do and he does it with the familiarity of task and skill he can bring to the job. He feels the smooth stem of his hammer, finds the nail required, perhaps plays with the head to gauge the size of the target of his swing. As he gathers up his tools of trade, he stiffens. He knows the disturbing feel of what is to come. He takes a deep breath to give him the looseness required for the job. Placing the nail to the wriggling palm he sets to. He must battle with struggling, moving flesh which must be impaled onto timber. It is here, in this scene of writhing, painful humanity that deliverance will come. Several bodies restrain the victim. They hold one man down, try to stop him struggling, while another, his hand to the mallet, drives the nails home.

These brutal fastenings make their presence felt more keenly as Jesus is hauled aloft. The full weight of Jesus' body tears at his hands and wrists. The final hours of Jesus' life are grim. The Master is unable to move without causing himself more pain or injury. Any move to ease discomfort anywhere in his body would have reminded Jesus that he was not free to move. Jesus was secured in a way which alerted his sense of touch to the fact that he was a prisoner. Any shift would have dire consequences. Yet the body automatically seeks relief. The urge to alter one's posture when uncomfortable is as routine as scratching when you feel an itch. The knowledge that the scratching may only inflame the irritation is momentarily forgotten for the immediate satisfaction of a good rub to the affected part.

Jesus is denied even such transitory relief. The three nails mean that any compensation of weight made consciously or unconsciously by Jesus would have sent unmistakable information through the body to cease, to try to avoid movement in order to place some limitation on the excruciating physical sensations. Any gesture would cause more damage to Jesus' already battered body.

It would be only a hardened spectator who could remain unaffected by the writhing of Jesus and Jesus' companions. Even if you averted your gaze you could hear the suffering in the cries and whimpers as Jesus hung on the cross. And such cries can cause automatic physical responses. Watching the nails pierce the flesh, you feel your own hands and wrists. Seeing the fall of the dead weight of the pinioned body as it is swung up on high, you push yourself up inside your frame. As the victim attempts to shift his position, your body moves, almost urging your muscles to provide some relief for him. But you know, for all your sympathy, that it is the one who hangs on the tree who really suffers. It is only his efforts which can result in relief.

In the end, Jesus gives up such efforts. Jesus is dragged down on his own weight. He cannot check it any longer. Jesus' breath catches. The very act of breathing can be felt. Jesus is pinned and can feel his lungs collapsing. It is from such agony that Jesus is called to save. The only possible release is a yielding to God, a yielding which gives Jesus escape from all bodily feelings:

"Father, into your hands I commend my spirit." Having said this, he breathed his last. (Luke 23:46)

EXERCISES

1. Start these exercises with two simple physical tasks, each lasting about five minutes:

- Sit as you would normally in any chair. Stay that way for some time until you feel you want to shift your weight or adjust your position. Try to resist the temptation to do so. Stay as you are until the discomfort tells you you must move.

- Move forward in the seat, removing all contact between your back and the back of the chair. Place your feet parallel on the floor. Close your eyes and concentrate on the length of your back. Let your back hold you. Try to feel what your body is telling you. If any stiffness develops, just breathe into it.

2. Form a fist with each hand. Clench your hands very tightly, closing your eyes as you do so. Slowly release them, opening your hands and eyes, saying, "Into your hands I commit my spirit."

3. Place the following objects in your hands. Feel them. Try to imagine something about them. Think what they tell you about the Passion. If you are in a group, pass them around. Resist the temp-

tation to talk about them immediately. Wait until everyone has sat with the object. Then discuss what you experienced.

- a piece of bread
- a glass of wine
- a piece of hardwood
- a nail
- a crucifix

4. Using a basin and a jug, wash your feet. If in a group, wash each other's feet. Allow yourself to feel the foot of the other person. Allow your foot to be touched.

5. If in a group, get everyone to hold hands. If alone, open your hands to the sky. Feel the air around your fingers. Say the Lord's Prayer.

QUESTIONS FOR REFLECTION AND DISCUSSION

1. The God-given sense of touch animates our lives in countless ways. As we give the following touches, what messages are we attempting to communicate? As the receiver of the touches, what feelings are evoked?

- a firm handshake
- a bear hug
- a pat on the forearm
- a gentle hand resting on your cheek
- a playful nudge in the ribs

2. As you imagine Jesus trudging wearily up the road to Golgotha, try to identify with the crushing weight of the cross Jesus felt against his body. Have you ever felt "the weight of the world on your shoulders"? When? How did it feel?

3. Suffering touches the heart of God—not only the suffering of Jesus, but our own as well. How can we experience God's compassion as real in our lives? How can we be vessels of God's comfort and compassion to others?

4. What do you imagine the disciples were feeling as Jesus washed their feet at the Last Supper? How would it feel to have your own feet washed by another person in a foot-washing service?

5. Not all touch is physical. We often speak of our hearts being "touched" by an inspirational story or beautiful music. What might it mean, then, to be "touched" by Jesus?

6. The author speaks of the casual contact of "brushing up against Jesus." In what ways do we do that today?

God, we thank you for the gift of touch.
We thank you for the opportunity to give and
receive through our hands, our bodies.

We thank you for the ability to communicate in ways
that need no words or sounds.
God who touches us, give us that sense which leads us
to closer contact with you. May we use this gift of touch
to reassure, to assist, to guide. Nudge us, urge us, shove us
along the path on which we can feel your presence.
May our hands feel for you.
May our lips smile for you.
May our muscles move for you.
May our bodies speak for you
the language of love. Amen.

Taste and See

"O taste and see that the LORD is good" (Psalm 34:8). These words from Psalm 34 at first seem to bring together two senses, the faculties of sight and taste. But what the writer is trying to express is not a confluence or confusion of senses. It is rather an attempt to deepen a single sensation. The aim is that by tasting we will *know* that the Lord is good. That taste brings knowledge. So he could render it: Taste and know that the Lord is good.

Despite claims to the contrary, we often hold ourselves back from knowledge. Such reticence can come from shyness. But it may be much more than that. It may be an honest acknowledgment of the way we are. It indicates our realization that we are not omniscient. We display this reticence when we concede that we cannot know everything. We speak of not knowing the full story. Paul uses the analogy of sight again when he says we cannot have comprehensive knowledge:

> For now we see in a mirror, dimly, but then we will see face to face. Now I know only in part; then I will know fully, even as I have been fully known. (1 Corinthians 13:12)

Paul casts that coming to a fuller awareness within the metaphor of growth from childhood. As a person grows, so does his or her knowledge.

As for knowledge, it will come to an end. For we know only in part, . . . but when the complete comes, the partial will come to an end. (1 Corinthians 13:8, 10)

We are faced with a dilemma. On the one hand, we are to think our understanding will grow with age. Wisdom comes with years. Yet we will realize that in the face of God our intelligence can be only partial.

This dilemma is central to our sensing of the Passion. Our working out of the suffering of Jesus Christ according to the senses insists . on the acceptance of this partial nature of our knowledge. Each sense provides an insight which contains material known through only that faculty. However, we can and do use data gained through one sense to apply for use in another. For instance, the sound of screeching car brakes can make us cry out or reach to protect a child or a loved one. The whiff of gas starts us in search of the source of a leak. That can finally be discerned by hearing. We hear a hissing. The problem is confirmed by the sighting of a rupture in a pipe.

Despite all this, we know that if we are to place all sentient experiences together, the result will still be only partial. We take on board the apparent contradiction that presupposes that a fuller knowledge than that we have now will come to us later. We know we must pass from the realm of the senses to new sense. We must wait until the end of our lives for completeness. That means we must acknowledge the conundrum that we cannot really know what lies ahead for us. Any knowledge that we assume will be complete may be so unlike our experience here as to be unrecognizable.

To a certain extent, the reverse of such thinking is also true. As mentioned before, the absence or the loss of one sense—sight, hearing, feeling, smell or taste—does not make a person any less a person. A person is a complete person whatever the state of his or her faculties. But by the rounding off of the five senses we can appreciate, we can see (as the psalmist says), the total sensual experience of the Passion. And the opposite is true. By losing those senses one by one, we arrive at the total obliteration of the experience of this existence. This is powerful for Christians. The shutdown of the senses in the Passion of Christ heralds the good news. The death of Jesus is also an event in which a new world and a new life are revealed.

Taste is the final faculty with which we will sense the Passion. Through it we will taste the final hours of our Lord. And by tasting them, it is hoped we will be brought closer to Paul's prediction. We hope that we will see more clearly. And through that we will know that the Lord is good. For the movement from the upper room to the road to Golgotha, to the nailing on the cross and to death is one that takes us from the savoring of taste to the loss of it.

Tasting the Goodness

Again, let us start with the Last Supper. How can we begin to savor the taste of the meal? It depends on the food. Do we take our cue from an artistic view of it, maybe as portrayed by the Italian master painters? There is a hitch here. The trouble is, what we often see depicted and thereby imaginatively taste is a meal that Italians would have had. Despite the tempting nature of that cuisine, it would be a fairly safe bet that a Jewish Passover held in Jerusalem would not look like the spread of the well-heeled Italian in the Middle Ages. The painting is done with the best of intentions. An artist is trying to bring the experience of contemporary viewers into an encounter with our Lord and the disciples. An immediate method of doing this is placing their world, in the shape of food, before those looking at the painting.

Yet we, who are trying to encounter these sensations so much later, have to insist on more detail. We have a difficulty here. It is a difficulty we acknowledged when we smelled the Passion. That difficulty is best expressed in questions. Are we in a position to know what food was available on the banquet table at the Last Supper? How far did the apostles insist on the observance of the Jewish food laws, given that Jesus and they had been lax in observing such strictures in the past? What tastes were part of the *seder* meal and what made up the subsequent feast?

Jesus had instructed some of the disciples to go ahead to a room and make ready for the Passover feast. Can we be sure that it would have been as prescribed by Jewish law and custom? We know that Jesus and Jesus' followers were not above bending the laws here and there. The gospels itemize several instances of this. They are criticized for not observing the ritual washing. They are accused of doing all sorts of activities on the Sabbath. These breaches of the law brought them into conflict with God-fearing and law-abiding Jews. Indeed, much of the gospel evidence for the prosecution and persecution of Jesus is that Jesus himself breached or incited others to breach the sacred nature of the Sabbath. Indeed, Jesus is quoted as denying the importance of the source of one taste, the flesh from animals.

> *"Do you not see that whatever goes into a person from outside cannot defile, since it enters, not the heart but the stomach, and goes out into the sewer?" (Thus he declared all foods clean.) And he said, "It is what comes out of a person that defiles."* (Mark 7:18-20)

One important part of the *seder* meal is what we would probably term the toasts. Four cups of red wine or grape juice are drunk to recall the blood which the Hebrews sprinkled on their doorposts to alert the angel of death to pass them over. These four cups mark the four stages by which Israel was delivered from slavery.

> *Say therefore to the Israelites, "I am the LORD, and I will free you from the burdens of the Egyptians and deliver you from slavery to them. I will redeem you with an outstretched arm and with mighty acts of judgment. I will take you as my people, and I will be your God. You shall know that I am the LORD your God, who has freed you from the burdens of the Egyptians."* (Exodus 6:6-7)

Despite the laxity Jesus and the disciples have shown, it would be safe to assume that at least part of the meal would be traditional. After all, they have gathered with the express purpose of marking the Passover. This most Jewish of Jewish feasts would have been celebrated as it is today. Along with any enjoyment or reminiscences brought on by the wine, their mouths would smart with the bitter herbs of *maror*. This tartness would be eased somewhat by the *beytza* (boiled egg). They could be invigorated by the spiciness of the *haroset*, the salad of apples, nuts, cinnamon and wine. There is also the special texture and taste of the *matzot,* the dry unleavened bread. Also there would be parsley or celery, dipped into the biting taste of saltwater.

There is plenty of time to savor these tastes because the *seder* meal progresses in stages. First, there is the identification of the food and what it symbolizes. Any symbolism, for instance the bitterness of slavery captured in the taste of saltwater, is explained as the meal continues. For those taking part, the consumption of the food is a sensual reminder of the trials and graces endured by and shown toward Israel. Those taking part in the Last Supper were renewed witnesses to what was already an ancient tradition.

For the apostles these tastes link them with their heritage. Having given up all to follow a person who so often upended their traditional values, they now share the table with their Master who recalls them to the basis of their faith. God loved the creation so much that he made it possible for it to be saved despite its own failures.

And, in a short while, Jesus was to turn this traditional meal into the forerunner of another symbolic feast which would become the focus of a new community. For generations to come people will gather to celebrate the presence of Jesus in their midst.

. We still have the problem of what sort of banquet followed the *seder*. We assume the food was celebratory. It probably would have consisted of what was available in the region at that time of year. However much the apostles enjoyed or failed to enjoy what was on offer, there is a vital change which overtakes this celebration meal. During their eating of it, tastes begin to grow bitter in their mouths. We know that this meal became an even more special meal than its supposed Jewish content would suggest.

> *Then he took a cup, and after giving thanks he gave it to them, saying, "Drink from it, all of you; for this is my blood of the covenant, which is poured out for many for the forgiveness of sins. I tell you, I will never again drink of this fruit of the vine until that day when I drink it new with you in my Father's kingdom." (Matthew 26:27-29)*

These words would have been the trigger for different reactions in the speaker and hearers. Jesus' throat dries as Jesus attempts to tell his friends that this meal is the last they will share together like this. Jesus' parched mouth is a presentiment of even more foul tastes that are to come. Jesus knows what is to befall him. Yet the Master's words wreak havoc around the table. Suddenly enjoyment of the food vanishes. Here, being passed around them, is a cup of blood. For the disciples there is an immediate taste of revulsion. We capture that in the expression that something objectionable leaves a sour taste in the mouth. Some of the apostles draw back. A tang of shock and revulsion in their mouths. Has the wine in the cup which Jesus has blessed and passed around really changed into the blood of their teacher?

Blood is life to Jewish people. One food law is that the life, the blood, should never be in meat when it is eaten. We feel the apostles' dry-mouthed expectancy, we watch the shaking of the cup as it passes from hand to hand. Our lips purse for a reluctant sip to share in what our teacher is trying to tell us. It must be an attempt. Because the apostles cannot know what it all means until well after the Passion unfolds. The expected enjoyment of the wine is now bitter. The cup seems full of poison. The taste makes some of them gag. They cannot swallow. They battle to control their disgust. No sooner has this been dealt with than Jesus reinforces his message.

> *Then he took a loaf of bread, and when he had given thanks, he broke it and gave it to them, saying, "This is my body. . . . But see, the one who betrays me is with me, and his hand is on the table. For the Son of Man is going as it has been determined, but woe to that one by whom he is betrayed!" (Luke 22:19, 21-22)*

For some this is easier. They have drunk and survived the cup. They are pondering the mystery of Jesus' words because it tasted just like wine. They eat the bread willingly. For others it is no mere morsel. Having lost the lubrication of saliva, the chewing is more of a battle. It becomes a painfully slow process to get the lump into a soggy mass which will still scratch its way down the throat. Questions arise. Did Jesus really mean what he said? Is it true that this bread before them is the body of their teacher? How could the wine really be blood?

We are faced with exactly that conundrum when we take part in Holy Communion. The body of Christ. The blood of Christ. That is what we say. Depending on your theology, we believe the consecrated bread and wine represents or that it *is* just that—the body and blood of Jesus Christ. And that through the Eucharist, Jesus is present in a particular way. It is in the sacrament of the Eucharist that we draw on the life of Christ. Being drawn into the life of Christ is a gift for us. But the gift is represented in Christ's blood, a thing prohibited to the taste of a Jew who observed the food laws.

What of Jesus himself? How did our Lord react to his premonition of his own end? Did the condemned person eat a hearty meal? Or did Jesus also find the food sticking in his throat? Did Jesus' knowledge obliterate the various flavors? Did the tension pall the sweetness? Did anxiety kill the savory? Did impatience neutralize tartness?

The Sourness of Anguish

In the garden of Gethsemane there are two tastes to savor. The first is that of the disciples Jesus takes along as he goes out to pray. As they take their places in the garden the taste of the meal remains. Its curious combination of ritual, pleasure and confusion is still on their palates. Perhaps overindulgence allows them to replay, without the initial consuming pleasure, some of the stronger elements of the meal when they belch. Yet we know the closing down of their senses, taste included, is imminent. Try as they might, the apostles cannot help but sleep. When Jesus rouses them, what do the apostles taste? Perhaps the scratchy mouth after a little too much wine. Or is it the solid flavor of a sleep cut too short? Is there a dry-mouthed resolution in their acceptance of the rebuke from Jesus? They taste shame because they know Jesus is right. They cannot stay awake and watch with the Master. Dry tongues try to provide some lubrication to give substance to their renewed alertness. But how fleeting it is. Jesus goes off and again the sense of taste fades out of consciousness.

And the Lord himself, choking back the anguish, asks for the cup to be removed. Having passed wine around among the disciples Jesus now uses the language of taste to portray his sense of impending doom. Here also Jesus is giving a hint of the last taste on his lips before his death. Drinking is, quite rightly, often seen as refreshment. Yet when a beverage is rancid, if it is sour, the body reacts to stop our swallowing it. For Jesus this premonition encapsulated in his prayer may have had a physical aspect to it. Our Lord may have been able to taste the bitterness of the cup which he is asking to have removed. Jesus was appealing not to have to taste it, but Jesus accepted the necessity of it.

Smells generate taste. So many of the odors of the Passion stories can be assumed to have a corresponding taste in the mouth of Jesus. Jesus would have tasted the sweet, the acrid, the pleasant and the unpleasant.

In another part of this book, we thought about the smells of the Passion. It is worth bearing in mind that taste and smell are closely linked. When I was a boy at high school we carried out a small experiment which involved trying out various foods on a partner. I will never forget holding my nose and closing my eyes while my partnered student painted my stuck-out tongue with a vegetable, and I hazarded several incorrect guesses as to what the vegetable was. When I released my nostrils I identified it immediately. It was onion. And I could not stand onion. The taste seemed to hang around for ages.

Jesus Tastes the Approach of Death

Much of the taste of what follows the arrest of Jesus in the Passion narratives can only be imagined. Some things do come to mind. We can assume that our own experience or knowledge may not be too far off the mark. The taste of fear is one we know from experience. Jesus is trying to swallow back the rising anxieties, disappointments and worries as the series of Jesus' trials takes place. Such concerns have a tang. Jesus goes before the high priest, Pontius Pilate, and Herod. This was a personal and stressful progression. In his silence before Pilate, Jesus, alert through noise, kept counsel with his own thoughts and taste. There is the taste of his tongue as Jesus keeps his peace.

This same member becomes vital as Jesus struggles to withstand the indignities undergone as a result of Pilate's order aimed at securing Jesus' release. As Jesus' body writhes in pain when he is flogged, so too Jesus' tongue jerks inside his mouth. Jesus holds back the screams. In doing so Jesus is forced to savor his own mucus and blood. Tears bring first themselves, then sweat, into Jesus' mouth. Finally a mixture of dirt, salt and blood is washed onto Jesus' own lips. The sheer intensity of these experiences is heightened when Jesus is forced to take the weight of the cross. Jesus' efforts to hold it aloft eclipse other sensations. The strain of making progress up the hill toward Golgotha renders Jesus unaware of taste. Jesus' mouth is too busy drawing in the needed breaths to sustain his efforts. Or Jesus is forced to blow his mouth clear of his own secretions.

The Stations of the Cross provide Jesus with a number of respites from the agonizing flavors of the Passion. The release is in the form of contacts with other people who are generally believed to be sympathetic to Jesus' suffering. When Simon of Cyrene is forced to take the weight of the cross, Jesus enjoys the taste of relative freedom. It is tinged with gall, because Jesus knows the reprieve is only temporary. Jesus' encounters with women likewise alter his sensual experience. Jesus speaks with his mother and to the women of Jerusalem. When Veronica wipes Jesus' face there is another brief moment of relief. Her gesture opens the pores of Jesus' skin. It also clears Jesus' nose. A sharper sense of smell brings with it a heightened openness to taste. This is fleeting, quickly replaced by what is to come.

No matter how heroic we consider Christ's action in accepting the will of the Father from Gethsemane to Golgotha, one taste persists. It is the taste of fear. Knowing the necessity or correctness of an action does not counter the natural shocks it causes. Several times Jesus has been redirected on his course and resignedly receives whatever is his lot. Yet the uncertainty creates a numbness tinged with fear. This numbness can be tasted.

All through the walk up the hill we can imaginatively place ourselves with Jesus. We walk with Jesus to the place where he is nailed to the cross. Jesus' mouth is parched. Its only relief is the taste of sweat, mucus and blood. This is a savage, raw experience. No more savage or raw is the moment when Jesus tries to taste his teeth, gritting them as the nails are driven into his hands and feet. Jesus' mouth reacts to each blow. First it closes. The lips form a vice-like grip. Then Jesus gasps to savor the air. Jesus seeks to breathe as much of it as he can to relieve the piercing pain. As Jesus is hauled aloft he finds in his mouth all the flavors of the day that has passed. They are intermingled, confused and confusing as Jesus tries to find some way to alleviate his suffering. The very nature of the event, the torture, the mocking, the carrying of the cross, all bring about bodily reactions which can be tasted.

But there is a special reason for reserving until last a consideration of the sense of taste in the Passion. That is simply that in the gospel accounts, taste is the last recorded sentient experience of our Lord. The experience of the torture, the carrying of the cross, the heat, the stress in the nailing to the cross, all would have had their dehydrating effect. Jesus' body was losing fluids rapidly through sweat, bleeding and other secretions. Jesus tasted the growing dryness of his body. This was communicated directly through Jesus' parched throat and mouth. Such aridity increases awareness of the tongue, which looms large and useless. It needs reviving. It needs assistance to go on, to slake the thirst, to flood the desert which Jesus' mouth has become. Without liquid our Lord cannot continue.

In a rare occurrence, all the gospel writers agree that the last sentient experience of our Lord was taste. The accounts vary greatly, as do the final words of Jesus before he dies. Yet it is a bitter taste which is the final element to enter Jesus' mouth. In John, we are told Jesus asks for assistance, having committed his mother into the care of the disciple whom Jesus loved.

After this, when Jesus knew that all was now finished, he said (in order to fulfill the scripture), "I am thirsty." A jar full of sour wine was standing there. So they put a sponge full of the wine on a branch of hyssop and held it to his mouth. (John 19:28-29)

The hyssop plant was used as a sprinkler in religious rites. This bitter taste in John is reminiscent of other bitter herbs in the Passover feast, Christ now taking the place of the lamb.

In the synoptic Gospels the same explosive bitterness is used in slightly different ways. Yet, whatever the account or the point being made, the taste is the same. In Luke's account, the offering is part of a larger insult.

The soldiers also mocked him, coming up and offering him sour wine, and saying, "If you are the King of the Jews, save yourself!" (Luke 23:36-37)

Matthew and Mark's accounts are closer to each other in what occurs to Jesus. The shock to his taste is a misplaced gesture of sympathy.

And about three o'clock Jesus cried with a loud voice, "Eli, Eli, lema sabachthani?" that is, "My God, my God, why have you forsaken me?" When some of the bystanders heard it, they said, "This man is calling for Elijah." At once one of them ran and got a sponge, filled it with sour wine, put it on a stick, and gave it to him to drink. (Matthew 27:46-48)

This last taste of the Passion was bitter indeed. The vinegar in Jesus' mouth was the taste before the end of all taste. When it had been experienced there came the end of earthly sensations—the end of the sensing of Jesus' Passion, and Jesus' sensing of life in this realm.

EXERCISES

1. Set a table with the following items from the *seder* meal. Take a small morsel of each piece of food and savor the taste of it in your mouth. Closing your eyes can help. As you do so, recall what they serve as reminders of:

- boiled egg: the roasted egg offered at the Temple;
- horseradish (bitter herb): bitterness and hardship of slavery;
- parsley or celery, dipped in the saltwater: reminder of spring, with the bitterness of slavery;
- *matzot* (available in many supermarkets and specialty shops): to recall the patriarchs;
- wine: symbol of the blood sprinkled by the Hebrews on their doorposts at Passover.

2. Imagine yourself in the upper room along with Jesus and the apostles. Think of your favorite food. See it on the table and bring the taste of its pleasure to your mouth.

3. Place some vinegar on a sponge or a piece of cloth. Read the passage from the gospel of Mark 15:33-41. At the end of the reading taste the vinegar on the sponge.

You may like to discuss your reactions to Exercises 1-3.

4. Think about and, if in a group, discuss the action of the Eucharist as experienced at your church. What symbolism is implied in the food and drink? What actions help your understanding of it? How important is taste to all of this?

5. If you meet in a group, try to arrange Holy Communion in the place you usually meet. Or go as a group to your place of worship. Sit together and partake of the celebrational meal in the company of each other.

6. Stand in a circle. Join hands and say either the Lord's Prayer or the prayer at the end of this chapter.

QUESTIONS FOR REFLECTION AND DISCUSSION

1. The significance of sharing meals together is emphasized repeatedly in the scriptures. Does our contemporary meal sharing reflect this sacredness? How is this practice honored in your home?

2. The familiar and beloved hymn "Blessed Assurance" speaks of a "foretaste of glory divine." How does our relationship with Jesus help provide this glorious anticipation?

3. Jesus' poignant words from the cross, "I thirst," are reminders of the urgency of thirsting—a symbol used in the Sermon on the Mount as Jesus urged us to "hunger and thirst after righteousness." How is this urgency reflected in our Christian walk? Does this intense yearning take priority in our lives—as if we were truly *thirsty?*

4. The author speaks of the "taste of fear." How do we recognize the taste of fear in our lives? In the lives of others?

5. As we experience the Lord's Supper, we are reminded that we are consuming Jesus' blood and body, taking the life of Christ within us. How can we make this sacrament more visceral, less commonplace? What techniques and ideas can we share with each other to enliven this sacred ritual?

6. During Communion, we are given both a sample and an example of what real commitment can mean. How is our taste for discipleship tested at the Communion table?

7. Has this study of the senses given you a deeper appreciation of the humanity of Jesus? As you focus on the fact that Jesus' five senses were operable as are ours, how does this change your relationship with him?

God and creator of all we taste, let us use
this gift to appreciate the blessings you have given us.
Help us to share our enjoyment of the gifts of
food and drink. Let us celebrate the range of tastes
we encounter in different cultures and cuisines.
Help us to remember that our taste is not the only one.
Dare us to widen our experience of the richness
you offer through the range of your people.
May we also use this sense of taste to ease
the bitterness of others.
We ask this through the lover of all and
giver of comfort, Jesus Christ our Lord. Amen.

One Body—
Bringing It All Together

Interestingly enough, none of the gospel accounts of the Passion includes nails. We assume their presence. We assume them because of the postresurrection appearance to Thomas. For it is Thomas who joins his experience, but initially his doubt, to these wounds. He brings his partial understanding to the others, but he is made whole by Jesus. As the result of touch Thomas moves from the cynical—

> *Unless I see the mark of the nails in his hands, and put my finger in the mark of the nails and my hand in his side, I will not believe.* (John 20:25)

—to a confession of faith. He moves from the event to its implication. At the appearance of Jesus to the apostles eight days later, the Lord invites Thomas to do what he has demanded as proof, to feel with his own fingers the scars left by the workman who secured him to the post. Thomas moves from his reasonable position of incredulity to a declaration.

> *Thomas answered him, "My Lord and my God!" Jesus said to him, "Have you believed because you have seen me? Blessed are those who have not seen and yet have come to believe."* (John 20:28-29)

For many disciples, including us who are separated from these events by time, it is not the experience of one sense alone which is important. It is how we bring together all our experiences in Christ. It is how Jesus has spoken to us or is felt by us in times of joy, sadness, grief or celebration.

When we set out on this series of meditations, I did warn that it was a non-sensical activity. We would look at the last hours of Jesus through only one of the senses. In the process, you may have felt yourself moved to consider part of the story in a different way. By pausing to look, hear, smell, touch or taste, you may have understood part of these final hours in a new way. Or you may have revisited some understanding of yours from of old but temporarily forgotten. Or you may have been confirmed in something you had realized long ago.

We are, of course, more than the sum of our senses. Losing one sense may be discomforting, even tragic, but it does not lessen our humanity. Disability does not disenfranchise a human's experience. At least, it should not.

Whatever or however you have been affected by exposure to part of the Passion, what is important now is the moving on. We are challenged to bring it together in our own lives. The power of the Passion is liberation. The irony is that this freedom brings us together. But we do not know of this until the events after Jesus is laid in the tomb.

The resurrection stories bring disparate elements together.

Jesus is seen again in human form. A person who dies is encountered again in various guises. Jesus is seen by them among them. Jesus is heard talking. Jesus eats and drinks with them. Jesus listens. Jesus touches and is touched, as we have seen in the appearance to Thomas. Jesus is felt to breathe and smell. And the effect is electric. The shattered disciples begin to recover. The disciples realize that Jesus has kept his word—that Jesus has come back after the destruction of his bodily temple. In Christ they become one. They start moving into a new body.

This triumph does not free them or us from pain. If God in Jesus must suffer the agonies of the Passion, it is clear God's followers cannot be exempt from suffering:

> For to this you have been called, because Christ also suffered for you, leaving you an example, so that you should follow in his steps.
>
> > "He committed no sin,
> > and no deceit was found in his mouth."
>
> When he was abused, he did not return abuse; when he suffered, he did not threaten; but he entrusted himself to the one who judges justly. He himself bore our sins in his body on the cross, so that, free from sins, we might live for righteousness; by his wounds you have been healed. (1 Peter 2:21-24)

The resurrection is the ultimate sign of grace. The disciples are reembraced despite their falling away in the Passion. Their failures, as individuals or as a group, are ignored. Jesus comes to them. Jesus commands them and promises them assistance to go about the business of being one body, the church. It is that body we are members of. It is that coming together which absorbs us and can help us to be of use. For that we must respect the various gifts, the individual senses, that each of us may offer.

By the Passion we are able to see ourselves in a new light. By the suffering of Jesus we can be agents of change, knowing that we are accepted and forgiven. This is available to all.

For just as the body is one and has many members, and all the members of the body, though many, are one body, so it is with Christ. For in the one Spirit we were all baptized into one body—Jews or Greeks, slaves or free—and we were all were made to drink of one Spirit. (1 Corinthians 12:12-13)